Expecting Teryk

Expecting Teryk

AN EXCEPTIONAL
PATH TO PARENTHOOD

DAWN PRINCE-HUGHES

Swallow Press / Ohio University Press
Athens

Swallow Press / Ohio University Press, Athens, Ohio 45701
www.ohio.edu / oupress

Swallow Press / Ohio University Press books are printed on acid-free paper ⊗ ™

14 13 12 11 10 09 08 07 06 05   5 4 3 2 1

Library of Congress Cataloging-in-Publication Data
Prince-Hughes, Dawn, 1964–
  Expecting Teryk : an exceptional path to parenthood / Dawn Prince-Hughes.
    p. cm.
  ISBN 0-8040-1079-X (cloth : alk. paper) — ISBN 0-8040-1080-3 (pbk. : alk. paper)
  1. Prince-Hughes, Dawn, 1964– 2. Parents—Biography. 3. Lesbian mothers—
Biography. 4. Autism—Patients—Biography. 5. Parenthood. 6. Pregnancy. I. Title.
  HQ755.8.A3 2005
  306.874'3'087—dc22

                        2005012369

For my sister, Davina

Deep in the brain where the memories lie
On the ghost of the earth
Lives the memory tribe,
There on the earth where the ancestors keep
The ghost of the earth
Alive in their sleep,
We dream of a past still alive in our flesh,
When the ghost of the earth
Was, in dream time, still fresh,
Our spirits recall the first and the last
As the ghost of the earth
Remembers our past,
The ghost of the earth shines pale and white
Soft colors of ashes
Glow quiet and light,
The ghost of the earth sees with grandparent sight
The mothers of fathers
Of children of night.

Contents

Preface

This book is the story of my thoughts, hopes, and dreams in the years—and then few months—before my blessed son came into the world. During this time, I remember looking for a book like this that might reflect my experiences and act as a mirror for my own fears, my own joys, my doubts, my own internal gestation. There were none.

First, there are countless books on the time right after a child is born, and I agree there is much that is poignant and marvelous to write about during that time; but there is something absolutely singular about the shadow time one lives between deciding to be a parent and holding one's child in one's arms. I have already used the word *gestation,* and I believe that that is what that time is, just as much for the parent as the growing child. I found this to be true for myself as my child took shape in my mind and I took new shape in my own soul. I have let the style of the writing in this book remain ghostly, waiting on the connections of the reader, like the salty soup of creation that takes form after thought. It dreams.

As a writer, I have enjoyed much success. Much of that success has been the result of my sharing my experiences as an autistic person, particularly in my memoir *Songs of the Gorilla Nation: My Journey through Autism.* In many ways I feel that this book is a child of that book, just as Teryk is a child of my life. Though I speak of his birth in *Songs,* I felt that the experience of becoming a parent was too large, too important an experience to leave on the few pages I have written about my son. He deserves my experience to be told in full.

The fact that I am lesbian also enters into my writing and always has. It is a casual thing to talk about for me, like all my experiences as a living person. In this book, the fact that I am with another woman takes on more importance, as it greatly influenced my experiences as a person who wanted to become a parent and had to cope with certain obstacles. So my sexuality becomes more prominent in the pages that follow.

It is my hope that gay and lesbian couples and disabled couples, people with autism and their loved ones, will find this work offers them something I couldn't find—a type of gazing affirmation of their own possibilities.

But I do not want to be known as an "autistic" writer or a "gay and lesbian" writer. I want to be known as a writer who describes and holds the human story. For that reason I have not set out to make this a book solely about gay or autistic parenting. People who are parents know that, ultimately, there is no such thing.

There is only parenting.

PART 0

Your Beginnings

My Life

September 25, 1995

Dear Teryk Brydanialun,

A gray and swirling mist moves over the daybreak field outside my window, still in shadow against the rising sun, and dances with its arms raised upward, like ghosts seeking the heaven of a new day, and I am here.

I'm not always sure what that means, being a ghost myself most of the time, but the me I think of here, now, is going to be your parent—or at least it is my silent and spoken prayer that it will be so. And so I send a silent and spoken prayer to your tiny spirit, wherever it is, and I tell your story, because it is my story, and that is how the big story is for parents and children and children who then become parents. Perhaps I will have become a child by the time you are a parent, and so I will tell you this story now, so that we can both remember it this way.

It may be true that I shouldn't be a parent and perhaps part of my writing is a journey through my own doubts and fears as much as it is a minted treasure reflecting my joy. I am damaged and healed and damaged again in so many ways and also plainly different in ways that have nothing to do with damage or healing. Many people have said that people like me shouldn't be parents. I will tell you what they say and what I have thought, too, because I have thought about all these things until they stretch back into my beginnings and I can't see them clearly anymore.

I want to tell you a story of your own beginnings. People have mostly forgotten the stories of their beginnings, and I want to weave you a creation myth, one that may help you remember who you are when the living seems hard or when you wonder about the world, as all born children do. So I sit before a notebook full of blank pages, its already-worn cover attesting to my intentions; I carry it as if it were you carried within my body, I hold this mostly blank book under my arm like a hidden splint for the broken wing of my spirit. I like to feel its familiar thickness next to my ribs, next to my heart. I carry it in a way that marks my belief that its pages and the waiting love it records will never be torn out and away.

They say that both children and books provide a certain kind of immortality. Maybe this is why parents often write books for their children even if they never write anything else. I have seen many books left for babies, often they are pink or blue, and they contain many facts but little context. I have wondered when in a child's life these books become meaningful for the child, or if they are more intended to be books of remembrance for the parents. This book I write for you grows up throughout its pages; it starts simply and grows more complex as it goes along, like you will. There will always be something in it for you. This book I write for you, my child, is meant to become meaningful to you when you have grown into the person you will become and to last until I have returned to be the ghost I was before I was born.

If we are attuned to a wider world where reality sleeps with its eyes open and speaks with its mouth closed, we see that living people are only nondescript shadows and disembodied voices; we are all immortal ghosts from before we are born, ghosts behind the illusion of living, and then ghosts once again when we die. I think, though, that our spirits stay the same the whole time. And so I write to your spirit now, and my spirit—and others—haunt this book; some of the ghosts within it are named and some unnamed.

Unnamed are you also, and I draw a black underline on the first white sheet, believing that the neat edge will someday support the letters that sum up my prayers, my life, my deep and pulsing desire to melt back into an older world, a more present wildness as I know a love for you that is as strong as time and gravity.

I would tell you where you began, but no one really knows where they themselves—or anyone else—begins. Sometimes people write neat stories and number each part with neat numbers, beginning, middle, and end, in sequence, on white paper and in black letters, as if stories really happen sequentially, predictably, in black and white. I would rather write parts of your story with colors that mean something, like the brown of memories and the red of birth. When you mix those two colors, you get the black of the words that go before and after their color, like the dark before and after our lives. It is what this book is made of.

I would rather use my favorite numbers, numbers I also see in color (3, 7, and 9), to write about my favorite person, and I can't think of any reason I shouldn't—as long as I remember that we all start and end at zero. In all the great creation stories there is a mysterious place where the beginning of the beginning begins in mystery. You started with the big bang or the small whimper of this great, vast universe; you started with our black and stone-grasping ancestors; many years later you started with my grandfather and grandmother, then with my parents, and you started with me.

I was born in a white room in a white hospital surrounded by the riot and irrepressible green of a land as hot and humid and ancient as the breath of dinosaurs, and when I left the white room in the white hospital I loved this green breathing with all my own breaths. As I grew I was unusual. I didn't let my mother hug me, and I ran away into the green to be alone.

Since I can remember—and that is a very long time—I have been pierced and pained by the loudness of life. There were many times as a child when I believed I would crumble in on myself, my emotional skeleton finally eaten away by the screaming and clutching of a society that dissolved me—normal life, other people call it.

I see the world in ways other people perhaps see it only in their dreams or their deaths, or maybe, like you, as they see it before they are born. When I write what I know—what is real to me—I am told that mine is a magical reality. I listen and talk to animals and rocks, and time is both action and peace, both a living thing and a thing that stopped before my own red birth.

Everything—from blackberry leaves to bends in streams—has a personality, a distinctness that invites friendly familiarity. My world is a place where people are too beautiful and too terrible to look at, where their mouths speak words that fall silent on my ears while their hearts break audibly. I sometimes wonder how the world avoids going deaf from the din of breaking and thrilling hearts and the roar of unshed tears and uncried joy. Instead, they grow in my memory, like a looping brown path that tells stories, and comprise it; it tells me anything can happen, anything could be true.

Some people call the way I am in the world *autistic*. Indeed, I have a piece of paper that says this is so. But I feel. I feel more than anyone knows.

Mine is a world of profound sensitivity, infused by the hum and cry of an ancient and archetypal way of sensing and seeing. I feel like the animal and the poet that bracket humanity's raw extremes, and just below the edge of my fluctuating consciousness are the voices of not only the present but the past—stretching back like mirrors reflecting mirrors with a chain of faces just beyond sight: the hurt of other children, the lostness and quiet contentment of animals, the growing things of the forest, the turning of space. All that has evolved. All that is wild.

When I was younger, I would sit at my desk at school or on the steps of my house and feel the eating away on the inside of me and the growing pressure outside—on my skin, my eyes, my ears—and wonder if I would just disappear. I was sure it could happen and would cry to my mom when I couldn't take it anymore. She would ask me what was wrong, but I couldn't speak it. She would resort to silently stroking my back, but I couldn't feel it; I felt as though I was made of stone and pain, as if my frame was a crying fossil, my mouth an ancient desert without sound.

Everyone worried about me, though I didn't understand that then. When I was older, a doctor told me the name for it, but I don't think they really know what it is, and that I am just me. I remember that I sat in the doctor's waiting room and read in a science magazine that two researchers had discovered that the mean color of the universe was beige, and I was more interested in the fact that this explained my affinity for that color and was the reason I collected beige things. Somehow this immense fact of the universe seemed more meaningful than whatever the doctor would say about me. Beige plastic figures made my mind swirl sweetly like tea with too much milk and sugar, beige walls reflected my body better than did mirrors, and beige buttons fastened me to a reality that otherwise flapped teasingly around me, bringing my inner, porous life together with the hollow howl of the peopled world.

I remembered going in to see the doctor and absently hearing the doctor tell me, with shallow finality, why I was the way I was. Asperger's Syndrome—a form of high functioning autism. But for me the words had had no meaning in the face of the beigeness of the universe and the truth that I knew: I had no boundaries, none of the walls that sheltered everyone else, everyone normal. I just am what I am. Though I guessed that other people might consider normal a beige word, I did not want it to be that color. This and a hundred other things made me sad or angry.

There were happy times, too, when I was a child and my way of feeling showed me heaven, and it is considered a well-known fact that children can't really understand heaven, but I did. Heaven was when I was on the lake with my grandpa, fishing for catfish and not catching anything but the sound of my grandpa's quiet humming. Heaven was when my grandma and aunt Virgie sat at the kitchen table and cut the tops off of strawberries from the garden and talked about the old days. I always wondered why they didn't mention me, because I remembered being there. I could see it in my mind as real as memory.

Heaven was when tornadoes were coming but we hid in the basement and played Yahtzee and ate cold fried green tomatoes and drank ice tea, because we knew the tornado couldn't get us there because the house was built by my grandpa—and God, as everyone knew, loved us. Heaven was waiting for us up above and out the screen door.

When I was ten we left the land I loved and my grandparents, who were a part of that land just as corn and fossils and thunderstorms were; it didn't matter if God was dark brown and could do anything, I had to go. I missed them and the land and sometimes I withered, as though I were corn torn from the field, a fossil put in a box, or a thunderstorm in the drying air, too dry for tears.

The only thing that could stop the chaos was the order of tiny objects —rows of pinecones and sticks on my windowsill, jars of bugs lined up perfectly on my shelf, and my own rocking. I rocked by going back and forth and I rocked by picking up stones; rocking, rocking, I became a rock. Stones became my own sediments, as old as ponds full of brown sand and green algae, reminding me, re-minding me to love. They reminded me to love as I grew into a young woman.

When I was a young woman learning about love, it happened that I loved differently than most people. Maybe it was because I was too sensitive, or too strange. This is a world fit for men, and men, for the most part, decide how it is likely to be. And, for the most part, I have always loved men and the things they create, thinking this a beautiful world full of beautiful things. But for some reason men haven't much looked at me, though I see in the mirror that I am beautiful. I think it may be that they see something that would take entirely too much time to develop, as this is a fast world. Or maybe they have seen that I am more of a woman's woman, and so it has been that women look at me and see what I see in the mirror. I have always loved them for that, because it is both in my soul and in my experience a wonderful thing to be beautiful to other women. It has shaped my life, and it feels like a very old way to be, part of an animal history. Like my autism, it has a fossil in the past of me, hidden, good enough just left in the dark, in the dust.

I remember, when I was a child I would hear the phrase from the Bible, the one admonishing us to keep faith with those who slept in the dust. I always believed they were talking about poor people, people who had no houses. Now I know that the words speak of those who have gone before us, who are now dead and buried in the ground. Even still, though I have the image of the dead in the dust, they are poor dead to me, and I keep faith with those who have passed before me because my family has been poor since my ancestors were a family, a poorness of coin as old as dust itself. I have little money.

In 1916 a scholar named Grant, a man who explored genetics, produced a book called *The Passing of the Great Race.* Using the same science that will make you possible, Grant came to the conclusion that the best of humanity was being corrupted by the raw stuff generating the birth of the poor, of the mentally defective, of homosexuals, of those different. Grant eventually co-founded the American Eugenics Society, which asserted that all such elements of humanity should be sterilized and, ultimately, eliminated.

Though many people would find these sentiments awful to contemplate now, the ideas are still offered. Whether they reflect the recent belief of James Watson, a co-discoverer of DNA, the basic building blocks of life, when he said that if there is such a thing as fate it is localized in our cellular nuclei or whether it is their own discomfort with the unfamiliar, some people would rather I had never been born than see me a parent.

Once, when I was learning about the sensitivity I have called autism, I found a small group of people who had been raised by autistic parents. I read every line that they wrote carefully, trying to see your future in their pasts. I was scared by the words they had written. They cited some of the features of autism—impaired ability to relate to others, narrow obsessive focus, the difficulty autistic people have in reading the needs of others—and offered it as proof that children should be protected from autistic parents with the strength of law. My heart broke as I read their stories. They suffered discipline too rigid and were neglected in body and spirit and socially isolated, bearing the brunt of attacks of rage, made to be silent for good and ever; they found they had no mirror, they were unknown. They were untouched. Later, when they tried to find out what was wrong with their lives, they were made invisible. Many lived lives of depression, feeling they had lost their childhoods and therefore everything after. They were frustrated because people blamed their parents' failures on their being damaged by the Great Depression, or being rural, or being immigrants, migrants, poor.

Could I do these things to you, I wondered? Could I ignore you when you cried? Could I forget to feed you? Leave you untouched? Attack you? Leave you with only the dismissal of others to act as your mirror for all that you had lost?

One man I read said that gay people shouldn't have children because defenseless newborn babies shouldn't have gayness imposed on them. He said that children of gay parents would eventually be teased by other children and the result would be that would be required to be ashamed of their parents. Being gay, he said, was as unnatural as orange grass or a green sky.

Would this be what I had done to you? Expose you to the meanness of strangers and friends? Expose you to a shame of me? Leave you curled on a distant patch of rusted grass under an unnatural heaven?

I haven't thought so. I have passed through these words and come to peace with a surety that I am not the person that stands in what these people have said. According to the National Resource Center for Parents with Disabilities, there are 9 million parents with disabilities in this country—15 percent of all parents. According to the United States Census Bureau, there are 601,209 gay families and 6,620,945 families in poverty.

Like all the children in those families, you will know sadness and maybe even desperation, you will know the pain of mockery and need of too many kinds to count, and the sting of childhood regrets. That is just what life is like, I think, and no one can stop it. Because beyond the sting and need there is always joy, there will always be joy for the soul who has wanted, who has grown.

I know in my shadows that you have something else, too. I can feel that you are wild. You will live, I believe, a persistent archaeology; a shard of sensitivity, a necroscopic examination of the born and breathing, a psychomancy in which you are the reader of your own reflection in the scrying pool. In your heart will be the archaic contents of our collective unconscious, reflecting as mirrors both dark and illusive and constantly awaiting perception. Everything that has ever lived will be inside you, and when you are an old man, covered by layers of sleep and time, the dust and cobwebs of a thousand needy things will throw a blanket over your memories and turn into rock as heartbeats slow and freeze. You will find you will understand everything, and understand it much better than I write it in these pages.

Expecting Teryk

And you will know hope. You will know hope as I have known hope. I have felt hope when I have seen the orange grass of fall when it goes to seed, ready to plant its future in the ground. You will know the hope of your ancestors' faith in the face of a tornado-green sky.

It is love that gives you hope.

Meeting Tara

October 3, 1995

You started where my own love started, and then you started where that love led—when I met your mother. I met your mother on July 9, 1994. Every child wants to know how his parents met, and so I will make this a part of the story now, for it is a beginning of its own and it made me believe in magic and mystery and all the things that bless beginnings small and large. It was a beautiful night, hot and clear. A light yellow sun was dipping in the sky over the water of the sound where I had lived and said goodnight to many endings. Seattle glittered in the setting sun.

During this particular July, I had finished enough school to get a degree. It wasn't easy, because I didn't like being around people very much and would rather have just felt the sounds of the birds that call, smelled the feeling of happiness like cut clover, and tasted the blackness and stars of night like most people taste white champagne with tiny bubbles. People, like too much blackness and calling, often make me want to hide someplace like the first place you will become a person—a floating, quiet darkness where one must search and strain to hear, to see, to feel.

I wanted to congratulate myself for staying in school. I had quit high school when I could no longer cope with the bright lights, the loud noises, the brilliant chaos there that other people think is normal. People thought I was stupid because I would hide, so I ran away to make them wrong. I had found a way to learn. It was a quiet way, like the quietness of the water as I sailed toward the evening.

I wanted to reflect on being who I was and decide what I wanted to do with my future. I bought a ticket for a boat cruise that would sail all around Puget Sound for an evening. I looked forward to watching the sunset on the water from the deck and looked forward to being alone. Took myself out to dinner on the waterfront and then got on the boat as the sun touched the mountains.

As soon as I got on the boat, I wended carefully through the strangers, not looking at them or letting them touch me, and went to the front of the boat where I could stand facing forward and see nothing but the water. There was just enough room there for me to fit in the snug point, and my mind and body thrilled at the sensation of having a tiny platform to stand on while water surrounded me on three sides, a trinity of holy motion, steady backwards, like the past.

I felt like I was the only one on the boat, and I liked that very much. I thought about when I was young and the good times, and the hard times, too, because I had changed a lot; I found out that I wasn't the only person in the world that was the way I was when I met and worked with gorillas in the zoo when I was in school. The gorillas told me that they understood what it was to feel too much and not be able to go anywhere, but they explained that you could still be happy, that life—wherever and however you live it—is something rare. I learned a lot in school about gorillas, but gorillas taught me about life. I thought about that as I looked out over the water and the mountains.

As we set out over the steel-colored water, I drank in the soothing taste of the warm yellow and purple of the sun coming to meet the chilled mountains and let the breeze feed me with songs that hadn't touched anyone but me.

People tried to talk to me, but I was short though polite, and soon I was really alone. Or so I thought for a little while. I was silently looking out over the water and thinking about my life. I felt proud. I had been through a lot and come out feeling like a chiseled piece of artwork—something beautiful after the pain.

Maybe it was the memory of the pain and the finding of beauty that made me feel her then. She was standing behind me, as silent as I was. When I turned to glance at her I saw silence and beauty and pain. I realized that she had been behind me for a long time; maybe for the many minutes we had sailed, maybe for the many years I had not seen her.

Her dark hair blew softly in the wind that had been singing to me, her face a little sad, her eyes far away. She was hugging herself against the air, which was growing cooler.

I thought about a story I had recently read about magical women who appeared to those who had strayed into wild places; beautiful they appeared, and surpassingly so, until they were kissed, whereupon they revealed their true appearance: shaggy, with enormous teeth, smelling of things ancient, coming from another time. Wild women, they called them in legends.

I watched her from the corner of my eye. Though she seemed cold she didn't move to go inside, where loud music was playing and people were drinking and dancing. I was having an argument in my head. I wanted to be alone. I didn't want to be alone.

Expecting Teryk

As I watched her I realized that even if she was a magical woman she was the kind that was beautiful and wild at the same time, perhaps one with sharp teeth and a soft voice, an unbound heart, a smell of old memories, a hair-covered beast, a naked breast.

Finally, I turned and said, "Do you have a coat?" It was all I could think of that summed up what I was thinking. I was worried about her; I felt that she was kind and sad and I wanted to offer her something to make her feel better, to feel seen and understood. And I wanted to talk to her. Another thing that is important to understand about me is that I don't think like most people, who find it easy to say something simple and appropriate when they want to speak to someone. I always make what people think of as the mistake of trying to say too much in one sentence and so it comes out not making much sense. Unfortunately, this makes them not want to talk to me, and so I try even harder next time to get everything into the first sentence I say to someone and it makes the problem become what is called a "vicious cycle." But this woman seemed to understand all that I meant. She smiled a little and said that she was ok. This is how I met Tara. We started talking and talked for hours about everything under the setting sun and then everything under the rising moon.

She was born in Akron, Ohio, and was raised in Kentucky and then in Idaho. She always read a lot and loved to be buried in books. She loved learning about the world, and that is probably why she went to school so long and then decided to teach other people just coming to college how to love reading books. But these things weren't as important as the secrets that she always wanted a horse but never got one and that she loved to draw but never showed anyone her pictures.

I was sad when the boat docked and we had to say goodbye. I am a person of sure extremes and would have been as happy as a simple animal if she had just followed me home, where we could talk until we ran out of things to say. But she left. And I left. It was that simple.

She called me on the phone several days later and asked me to spend time with her again. I worried about our first date. There are a lot of things to remember. For example, the tenets of romantic gifts are not always tenable; giving lunchmeat on a first date is considered inappropriate, no matter how much the recipient might like lunchmeat and regardless of the fact that such a gift conveys your ability to provide. Giving flowers is considered appropriate with good reason, since they were originally used medicinally, which intimates your wishes for the good health of your date. However, giving someone wildflowers that you picked on the way to the date is considered "cheap," even though the flowers are more likely to have greater medicinal value than a store-bought bouquet. Either way, the polite thing to do upon receiving flowers would be to eat them, but that isn't considered appropriate either.

Despite all such potential pitfalls, we ended up spending a lot of time together. She was a simple animal, too, and we still haven't run out of things to talk about.

I loved Tara because she loved animals, because she was gentle with people, because she tried to understand things from all different sides. She is one of those people who have what is known as "an embarrassment of riches." She is smart, sensitive, funny, well-educated, caring, and warm. She understands people in ways that mystify me. She can make them feel at ease before she even speaks to them, and people are drawn to her. She got me to eat new food, and that is saying something, since every single day for three years before we met I had a shake for breakfast, two servings of ramen during the day, a salad for dinner, and popcorn for bedtime. Sometimes I went out for dinner and had something else, but that was rare.

I had another great surprise. Because something else that is different about me is that I don't see people's faces very well until I get to know them. Imagine my delight when I was looking at Tara after we had been together awhile and suddenly realized she was beautiful as well. Even my grandpa said so.

The Dream

I had a dream. At first it was painful because it was about my grandpa, whom I loved so very dearly and who died a month before I met Tara. In the dream I was sitting with my grandpa at the end of his kitchen table, a very important place to him because food, as far as my grandpa was concerned, was love. His table fed me, and at the head of it he said prayers of his own at every meal, and it didn't matter what the words were that he said to Jesus, they were about me. I understand this now that I have come to pray for you; for everything a parent says is a prayer for her children and her grandchildren and her great-grandchildren. Parents say them through open and closed lips and through their walking on the earth and at their tables. It's how we are fed.

This is how I sat at the end of the table with Grandpa in this dream. At first it was just a dream—the kind that is just on the edge of a nightmare because you want to cry, maybe you don't even know why, and that need to cry wakes you up a little and the dream is a dream, edging away from nightmare, because you know it is something else, something more real than being awake. When I realized that I was dreaming something more real than being awake, my grandpa smiled at me. I looked over and realized that Tara was sitting at the end of the table with us. She was smiling, too.

My grandpa winked at me and said, "I had to look through a lot of pretty girls to find this one for you."

He put his hand on my knee. I felt it. He was there. I wanted so badly to hug him and tell him I knew he was dead, but the dream was fading into something less real and I woke up with tears and my grandpa's smell on my face. Tara was lying in my arms.

When she wasn't in my arms, Tara wrote me letters.

August 18, 1994

"I finished reading your letter. I laid down on your blue shirt, smelling your warmth and letting my feelings for you wash over me. I sit here in the dusk and I can't shake the feeling of a destiny starting to unveil itself. I've been afraid that falling in love would drain me, sap my strength, but today I feel stronger because I feel you inside of me. I feel like I can almost touch you. I feel your energy around me and I feel safe, loved, protected. You believe in me and you help me find my own courage. This is the first time since I was a very little girl at my grandmother's that I've known someone was behind me, hoping the best for me, waiting to help if I need it but leaving me free to find my way, take my first steps across open space. I know that with you I will enter territories that are unfamiliar and perhaps for that reason frightening. But I will enter them anyway. I trust your heart and your intentions.

I want you to guide me, and I want to find paths that you and I can explore together. My instincts have led me to you; I will not doubt them again. I feel hopeful about our future together. I think about our work together, years of growing with each other, growing into the soil. We have so much time—we have most of our lives ahead of us. What a miracle that we met now, when the time is right for both of us. Thank you for your friendship, your affection. Tara"

October 26, 1995

I got up this morning as the first beams of the sun came through the window, and I stretched long and hard in the light. I reached into the closet and lifted out the tidy stack of clothes I prepared last night, as I always do. After I took off my underwear, which I wear only to sleep in, I shook out my standard uniform and got dressed. Beginning with my thick, white socks, I luxuriated in the feeling of their soft cleanness as the material encased my feet and calves. After that I slid into my baggy jeans, which I never put into the dryer. I like for my pants to be able to stand by themselves; it makes me feel like they are a real, solid body encasing me when I put them on and they stand stiffly out from me, providing form and boundary. I slid on my heavy boots so that my socks wouldn't be in contact with the floor, where there was risk they would get dusty and lose their magic. Next I pulled my oversized, black cotton tee shirt over my head and tucked it in haphazardly. I ran my fingers through my hair until it felt right. I didn't look in the mirror; I don't like looking into faces if I don't have to, even into my own searching eyes.

I moved to the sink and wet my aquamarine blue toothbrush—the brand and color I have always selected since I was a child—and shook out some Colgate tooth powder from the canister that sat on the shelf, making sure none fell off the stiff bristles of the brush I held carefully at eye level. I consciously brushed each tooth surface and ended my morning routine by spitting in the sink and rinsing all traces of the swirling white foam down the drain.

Ready to write, I lifted my battered old jacket from the peg where it always hangs, sliding into its warm and familiar embrace, like a second skin or a first, before tucking your book under my arm and stepping through the open door that led out to the great, noisy world.

As I stepped out into the growing green, the remembering brown, the singing palette of this season, I greeted them all quietly in my way. I always allow them to reach inside my chest, inside the folds of my brain and my smooth muscles, inside my spongy breathing and the contraction of my bowels, to wish them a good morning. I greet them all separately: each color and plant, each animal unto itself, and then I greet them as one thing that includes my own body before I start on my walk through it, through myself.

I can't remember how many days I have started down the trail for my secret writing place. As I strode through the early morning sun my steps walked backward in my memory. I had walked the trail at least three times a week for three months and two weeks. As I thought about the numbers I saw them in color. I calculated. Each trip was three miles (I had driven to different places in the car to find one that was at a distance that corresponded to one of my favorite numbers). *14 weeks x 9 miles = 126 miles,* I thought in color. Working my mind unconsciously, I added the numbers of the final sum. $1 + 2 + 6 = 9$. I was filled with numerical ecstasy as I realized that one of my favorite numbers, 9, was associated with this particular walk and with this particular entry in your book (my only regret was that 7 hadn't been any part of the equation).

To celebrate, I counted my steps by nines, adjusting them when I neared my destination so that the series would be complete.

As I walked I thought about the word trail. I said the word itself, silently, in nines, in time with my steps. Trail is a brown word, and I have always thought of it as a blending of *trod* and *tail;* the word evokes images for me of a wild and content animal on its right path, looking for what it has already. Thinking the word as I counted—trail-trail-trail-trail-trail-trail-trail-trail-trail—I strode down the trail like a happy dog. It reminded me of dusty trips, of the hungry grind of gravel, of the thirsty sun overhead.

☙

Almost exactly a year before I started this book, Tara and I took a trip. It was an important trip, because it is another place that you started. We drove from Bellingham, Washington, all the way to San Antonio, Texas. We put five thousand miles on the car before we got back home because we didn't fly there like crows are said to, in a straight line, but wandered around like ants looking for sugar and so we found a lot of sweet things.

One sweet thing we found was that the desert is haunted by a million ghosts who leave the spirit of honey everywhere. Sometimes this honey of phantoms feeds people, sometimes it burns, like fire made thin and running.

There are spirits in the hovering dust, distorted and hot, shimmering, smokes puffing in the heat, graveled and sizzling. There are spirits in the cracking cairns and the pungent incense of a long season of summers that relish your juices and ask you to bask in their warm embrace, feeling the long, dry sleep of mummies. There are the spirits of saguaro cactus and chollas, sagebrush and ground-crawling limoncillos and magenta-colored windmill flowers. Sometimes things that are still alive become ghosts because they live so long they forget the difference between life and death, like the two-hundred-year-old saguaro cactuses who were seventy years old before they even grew an arm—waiting another seventy years for the one still missing, like the ghosts the Assyrians called *utukku,* who were missing limbs and could cause illness and waylay travelers.

It has been so hot, perhaps so cruel here for so long that Joshua trees have grown long green arms imploring the sky for rain and cool, aware that

Expecting Teryk

they are surrounded by creosote bushes that poison the ground and kill their babies so that only the ones far away survive. Perhaps the Joshua trees have tormenting visions like the Desert Father Saint Anthony, who, in the stygian heat of conviction, wandered alone for years, hearing only his own voices. Surrounded by the desert I imagined his solitary mass, the ghosts around him, unheard as they answered in soft, gray whispers . . .

"Eternal, blessed Holy Ghost . . ."

"A thousand souls within one host . . ."

"The world is joyous in its praise . . ."

"Sing songs of death, the dead to raise . . ."

"We ask forgiveness for imperfection . . ."

"In death we see our own reflection . . ."

"With humility I ask for cleansing . . ."

"Through the soil binding, mending . . ."

"I admit that I have sinned . . ."

"We let the veil, gray descend . . ."

"Bring me to eternal life . . ."

"An end to fear, an end to strife . . ."

"I beg for entrance to your holy domain . . ."

"And there, and here, we shall remain . . ."

"For you are the life and resurrection . . ."

"The spirit of eternal connection . . ."

"The dead will dwell within your house . . ."

"A deeper place to hear our vows . . ."

"This bread is now your broken frame . . ."

"A spirit to feed all the same . . ."

"Give life to all here and departed . . ."

"Together, whole, and heal-hearted . . ."
"Bless this cup, a blood salvation . . ."
"Redeem us from our separation . . ."
"Bless this cup, life everlasting . . ."
"Blessed is our final passing . . ."
"Lead me not to stray and fall . . ."
"This desired by one and all . . ."
"In remembrance of thee . . ."
"Remember no one, remember we . . ."

Saint Anthony lived on three olives and a piece of bread a day, praying for his Lord to come and get him, not seeing that the lord was under his feet and never knowing that if he had listened to the whispered words, they would have made a better prayer than his own.

For the desert is heaven, too, and when its ghosts see apparitions, they are the spirits of the unborn and not the dead; I believe they show them to us in the cactus wrens who build nests for their babies among the great needles of the cholla and make it a safe place for little ones to grow, and the ghosts of the desert show us hope in the nursing palo verde trees who nurture the baby saguaro, offering them shade and protection from the cold.

It was in this desert of the ghosts of the passed and the waiting that you came into my body, let me build you a soft and safe home inside my sharpness, let me shelter your tiny spirit from the cold.

I think it happened as Tara and I drove down the dry New Mexico highway through a famous field of acres of satellite dishes cocked to the sky and listening for the ghosts of space. I looked over at her, driving quietly, the wind playing with her hair, her lips dry from talking to me about my dreams, and I was filled with love for her. I felt it welling up in me and I

Expecting Teryk

tried to let it out by saying it out loud, perhaps thinking it would leave my body on my breath, my spoken words. "I love you," I said. Tara said, "I love you, too." Tara smiled at me and then turned to watch the road. Her words filled me once again. The idea of you started growing somewhere inside me. This was an odd feeling for me, because, being born without a body myself, I didn't know where to put you.

Tara and I laughed about it, because I was suddenly getting cravings and would make her stop in strange places so that I could buy non-alcoholic beer and liquid amino acids and drink them together. I wanted enchiladas for almost every meal. I gained weight and felt like laughing because the stars were in the sky and crying because the sand was at the side of the road. Some people would have called this a "false pregnancy." But I think that if your body wants something so badly that it makes it happen, that that is as real as anything gets.

I felt you growing in me, and so did Tara, because we knew it was an idea and ideas themselves make things happen. The idea of making you grow made us very happy, and that's real, too. So it was a real pregnancy and I will always feel like you came through my body first, your little spirit telling me that you wanted to be born, before you came through Tara.

And so, in the birthing heat of a land that is never as barren as it looks from far away, we drew nearer to asking you to come to us.

Tara and I talked a lot about why we wanted a child. I know some people want children to make them feel immortal, or so that their children can "have a better life" than they did, or maybe because they want their children to do things they wish that they themselves had done but had not. I wanted a child because I believe life is the best phenomenon I have ever heard of—could ever dream of. When you are lucky, one chance in millions makes you start to grow, and when you think of the chances in millions that a million of your ancestors had to have for you to be here it is easy to think that it is impossible that you are here at all. I wanted to have a child to honor those one-in-a-million chances of being a human being on this earth, at this time, to look up at the stars and fill your lungs with breath, to count the agony and beauty of love and looking. Tara felt that way too.

There are a lot of questions hopeful parents have to ask themselves before they have a child. We asked ourselves what kind of parents we would be. What would be important to us about rules and beliefs? What would we tell you about God, about your family, about everything? We agreed that we would be honest when you asked questions, that we would make sure there are no final answers to anything, and because being right is, to a large degree, dependent on context, we would let you eat chocolate before break-fast as long as you were nice to people and searched for the truth, knowing you would never find it. We agreed that we would hug you a lot.

But those were all the things we decided we would do after you were here. Getting you here was a more immediate problem and we talked a lot about how you would come into the world. There are a lot of decisions we still have to make and lots of challenges to overcome to get you here. I will talk to you about every step as I tell your story in this book. Even now I feel your little spirit looking over my shoulder as I write, and I love you already. Starting from now it will never matter if you are asleep, if we are far apart, if we fight or disagree, or if one of us is in the world of spirits, I will love you, always, all the time, forever.

PART 3

Your Family

When I Married Tara

June 28, 1996

Tara and I got married today. It was our way of sharing with everyone the fact that we want to be a family and stay near each other always. Both our families and all of our friends came. Everything was decorated in peach and white and the taste and smell of peaches still fills me as I write this.

We stood in front of everyone and told each other, and them, how much we loved each other and never wanted to go away from each other. We asked our family and friends to help us be good to each other, to be strong for each other, and to share our happiness.

Some people think that marriage is mostly about finding a permanent person to have sex with, and I remember that through my life I have gotten the message that sex and marriage were two sides of the same coin. But I did some calculations.

I figured out that after two years together, Tara and I have spent about 8,850 hours together. Of this, we have spent about 150 hours making love. That means that about 99 percent of our time spent together, our relationship, is companionate and has nothing to do with sex.

Perhaps I couldn't have it any other way. From the time I was small I have found it difficult to be surprised by the casual touch of people always in my mind and heart, so much a part of me that their touch can be painful, reminding me that they are not me, but another. Sometimes I feel prematurely old, finding that Tara's look from across the room, her setting tea down by my elbow, her movement beside me in sleep, is enough. Today, though, I feel young and open.

We celebrate our union. Wine and laughter flow freely on the day of our wedding. I see the flush of my father's cheeks as he raises his happy glass. My mother sings loudly songs she had forgotten until the ghosts of grapes and sunshine brought them back. Tara and my sister chuckle at life with bright smiles and bright eyes turned toward the happiness of this day. Our friends make toasts and bawdy jokes. It is a bacchanal in the true sense of the word, and I think of the Greco-Roman wildman Dionysus, the god of wine. In the sixth century, his short, pug-nosed, hairy figure appeared in Athenian plays, replete with large, flexible phalli: he was a god of excess and of lust. But he was also a God of progeniture—the quiet after the rage, the passion.

That is what marriage is. After the celebration, after the dizzy extremes of intoxicating desire, it's about being with one special person, sharing the mundane things in life: work, doing the dishes, feeding the pets, paying taxes, sleeping, eating, laughing, crying, spending time with friends and family, getting sick, getting well, raising children—a family. That will be a long celebration.

Grandma Joyce

When I think of your Grandma Joyce, my mother, it makes me think once again about the strangeness of beginnings and the ways that time is a different thing when you are talking about someone you love. It seems strange to me that I remember my own childhood, back to my own birth it seems, and yet I remember the color of my favorite blue baby bottle much better than your grandmother's face. There are pictures of her that stand out in my memory: she is holding me while we wear matching blue suits, her hair a perfect sweep of blonde and her makeup flawless; she is rocking me and singing me to sleep when I am sick, I hear a plaintive wheeze from her dogged asthma as she intakes a labored breath between verses; she is bending over me, peeling a banana as I stand in my turquoise walker and look over at someone taking a picture of us together—I remember thinking to myself that I would remember the moment the picture was taken, even though it was before I could walk. I have remembered.

I have known for a long time that other people don't remember little tiny things the way I do, crisply, sharply, painfully; it is as if I could fall on my memories and give myself up to them as if I were falling on my own sword, falling into memories through the cut, to disappear into the past. Other

33

people forget the tiny things of the kind that make up my life and remember the larger ones that they believe make up their own. Your grandmother, who no longer wears makeup, no longer cares about the big world, is no longer mindful of human events, is caught between these two ways of remembering. They say that my kind of sensitivity comes down through families, and so it is in your grandmother, a living tracing of a time when people weren't given labels for the oddnesses such as she has, for better or worse.

She lives on a mountain alone, far from any human people, surrounded by the squirrels and deer and bears that have become her memories. They have become her friends, and she has no others. She has learned how to give mouth-to-beak resuscitation to the little birds who sometimes fly into the big windows of the house, and she saves many of them this way, holding them in her hands and blowing lightly over their tiny nostrils until they revive and leave her hands for a longer life. She saved a wild bunny with a broken leg. She trained her to use a litter box and kept her from jumping on the furniture by using a technique she called "pillow hawk," which took advantage of Missy Bun's natural fear of things passing overhead as she swung a cushion from the chair over the rabbit's head in a fast curving motion. Despite the coronary stress this must have caused her, Missy Bun stayed with us for ten years, hopping around the house until the day she lay on her side, breathed hard for a few hours, and left the house on the mountain behind. Part of my mother went with her.

When my father discovered a nest of squirrels in the side of the cabin, my mother made him build a ramp from the hole in the house to the nearest tree to facilitate the squirrels' travels between the forest and our house. When the winter was hard one year, she bought vitamin blocks for the deer to lick and put in a heated bucket near the house and shoveled a trail to it, clearing the snow for them each day. When a bear came and tore down the bird feeder to pull out the sunflower seeds, she placed the feeder higher and felt sorry for the hungry bear.

I think the animals know about your grandmother and your grandmother's house, and so they go there. They remember, too. And so, on the calendar by the phone she never uses, she remembers for them and for herself, and without knowing it, she writes beautiful poems about the small things that make up a life and are preserved in small squares under the headings of January, August, and October.

August 12: The wounded deer is back. The cat killed one of the baby robins from the nest on the porch.

October 13: Took down the hummingbird feeder today. Heard a bear on the porch last night, the cats' food is gone.

December 4: Saw a wolf on my way to Whitefish today. First one I have seen, not just heard in the distance.

The things your grandmother sees and hears from a distance are made of the same homespun cloth of vision as memory is itself. She told me a story once. While she was pregnant with me, she shook hands with President John F. Kennedy. She said he reached over two lines of jostling people to take her hand in his own. She said that when their eyes met, they both knew something, but that's all she could say.

Once, I was in a motorcycle accident that left me struggling back and forth, in and out of consciousness. I was dreaming that I had gone home to my parents' house. Feeling fuzzy and confused, in my dream I was telling my mother, who was sleeping in her bed upstairs, what had happened. My mother was, in fact, sleeping in the house I was dreaming about at the time. She, in turn, was dreaming that I came home and was telling her about the accident, speaking slowly and strangely.

Later, when we talked about the accident, she said she knew I couldn't die because my work on earth wasn't finished yet, that I was going to do something important. I think that the important thing I had to do was bring you into the world.

Teryk,

I hope I will always be near when you need a helping hand. You will have to teach me to be a terrific grandmother. We can learn together.

I wrote you a poem:
Roses are not consistently red,
Violets are not consistently blue
But my sweet, wonderful grandbaby
I will always consistently love you!

Grandma Joyce

Grandpa Ron

July 26, 1997

When your Grandpa Ron was a very young boy, he read a little book called *Miss Pickerell Goes to Mars*. The book was about a very organized and predictable old woman who, quite unexpectedly, climbs into a rocket she finds in her wheat field one day and streaks off to pay a visit to the red planet. Since then, your grandpa has dreamed of flying away. On the breeze that he shut his eyes and dreamed would bear him away as he jumped off the garage with a sheet tied at his wrists and ankles was the smell of too much alcohol and too many screams from the house below. He jumped from time to time, as a very small boy, waiting for the screaming and stinking wind to turn light and smell of space, but it never did, and each time he jumped he fell, getting a beating for ruining the sheets.

When he got older, he realized that he could go anywhere in his mind and wherever he went in secret, in the folds of a mind waiting to fly away, he wouldn't hear anything but his own voice, he would see only the beauty of his dreams. It was your grandpa's secret dream to be a writer, or a painter. He was good and when he wrote or painted everyone could see that he could be those things, that he was those things even then.

He and your grandma loved each other very much. They met in junior high school, and your grandma and grandpa never loved anyone else from that point onward. Grandpa Ron would write and paint for Grandma Joyce. When they were nineteen they got pregnant and had me. Grandpa Ron put away his paints and stopped writing. He loved me, but he was mad that he would never be a writer or a painter. When I got older, we fought a lot about it, without knowing that that was what we were fighting about.

But when I became a writer, he wasn't angry anymore and I wasn't angry anymore either, because the writing was getting done and it doesn't care who writes it. I knew it didn't belong to either of us, but to all of us, and I thanked him.

I took him to New York City to see his favorite painters. To my father, going to the Metropolitan Museum of Art was a holy pilgrimage, and I watched his eyes as we climbed the many steps. He looked like Moses. We went inside, where it burns.

He wandered, feeling lost. His mind tired and his body weak from years of not being here, in this place, he tried to draw strength from the familiar paintings, ones he had seen in his books all of his life, as a very old and scaled creature might draw life from the waited-for sun. There were times he dreamed that he was walking around in his own work, itself so familiar and unpainted, and there was some distant comfort in hearing the mute building, the frames, in seeing light and shadow and color and in tasting the dry rock of freed statues and the powder of dust, now settled into the shapes of love and loss. He sniffed the air for time, but it was not there. There was nothing to count, nothing to divide into manageable bites, nothing in sequence to give context to what was happening to him.

Avoiding the streaked and bleeding people who passed by him unseeing, he forced his steps, as if he were swimming upstream, to go on and on and seek the source of his birth. He allowed his mind to let go, and I silently followed him. The amorphous walls were adorned with clear and distinct paintings, like so many clear and staring eyes. The paintings and your grandfather stared at each other. He let his gaze rest on each painting in turn, only here able to meet the returning gaze without turning away. He let the paintings look at him. He didn't apologize for his life.

From one intense, framed eye a black forest brooded under a red sky as two tiny figures, almost invisible, walked almost unseen among the dark roots of the sunset painting. We sat on the bench together to look at it. Your grandfather lifted his own eyes and returned its scrutiny. Your grandpa closed his eyes, feeling peace. He himself became as simple as the landscape as its simplicity enfolded him.

As the relentless dark of the rendered sky armored him and made him naked, he let the still vibrant colors of his soul spill out into the air, into the ground, into the sky, caressing his sore chest, lifting and fluttering his bruised belly, probing and medicating the folds in his head, like a baby turning in its mother.

Beside him, I closed my eyes and reflected on the feeling of being wrapped up in the person beside me; it was not as painful this time. I imagined the sunset, the trees, the painting, my father. I felt a vision wash over me, a dream of leaping stags and lumbering mammoths. My own limbs suddenly felt like joints of meat ready for a swell of fire, a ripple of consuming smoke. He dreamed, he awoke, and I dreamed again as he thought of the painting. We were old together.

Our culture was the first to make tools, to see that the mind could shape the world, to make tools and then to make the tools of music, of art. Drums in our minds, string quartets in every breath; the raw heartbeats of foot on path and the silent arias of slippery things trying for an untried shore. And the tools of brush and knife, to make worlds where thinking made tools, and art, a culture of invisible trade. It was a trade our ancestors made well. A culture of the human family, an equal trade; invisibility for tools and art, a trade of life and death.

When I was a child I talked to the ancestors all of the time. They told me that it is the secret wish of all the living to connect with the dead, and the never secret wish of the dead is to learn from those who lived before— to become old ghosts and wise. And so the living learn from the ghosts they can understand, as do new ghosts, and new ghosts becoming old learn from the animals, and the ghosts of animals learn from the ghosts of lizards, who in turn learn from the ghosts of fish who learn from the ghosts of water. After that? Ghosts of the water learn from time, which has never lived but has always been a ghost. These are the things I learned from the ancestors. I suddenly realized that my father had known this all along.

Dress in the sparks of a million years,
Dress in the rain of a million tears,
Wrap yourself in your ancient kin,
Living in the colors of their ancient skin,
Its scent comes down from a wind on high,
Dress in the breath of the spirits of the sky,
Hide yourself in the memories of those who died,
Those who remember the skin of the tribe,
For we are all the same from behind our eyes,
All are dressed in time, where colors never die.

I opened my eyes. I turned to look at the person beside me in the gallery, my father, suddenly a stranger. I smelled the living smell of the bursting trees and the distant smell of living water. My father's eyes were closed and he looked as though he were thousands of years old. I imagined that if I could see inside his skull, that there, on the inner wall of his sealed head were cave paintings; prancing ponies, old bulls full of life, the rocky horns of aurochs, imprints of unseen hands in halos of color, words I couldn't read, circles of red that led nowhere, and crouching lions around a holy man. There was an echo inside my father's head. It sounded like God's second thoughts.

Perhaps the ghosts of our ancestors paint in spirit colors, and they leak into memories, causing madness. Perhaps that is their way of healing the ones held dear. My father opened his eyes. We were silent together. Then I asked,

"Why are picture frames always square?"

He said, "It's because most people like predictable boundaries."

"Sometimes I wish I had predictable boundaries," I said softly.

Your grandfather laughed. I couldn't tell if he thought I had made a joke or if he really understood what I meant.

"But I don't. Neither does anyone else," I said.

"That's how life is," he said.

The colors around us suddenly seemed to blow, chasing an unseen wind.

A museum attendant came by and told us that the building would close in ten minutes. My father didn't say anything, but I could tell that he felt pinned down by time once again, and it wouldn't let him up. I wondered how much time he had spent being uncomfortable in exactly the way he was now. The clock in the hall ticked. It was the institutional variety that had a stern and authoritative second hand that marched like a fascist army across the softer lives that consulted and feared its message. I wondered whether, if the clock were to suddenly stop, my father's discomfort would go away.

The clock didn't stop, and he took a last deep breath, trying to suck in the peace of the painting before him, to carry its exquisite aloneness into his chest where it could replace the fast beat of his heart with the slower rhythms of grass and water and bare trees. He rose and crossed the room, crossed its threshold, and began the repetition that led his footsteps back to his regular world.

Now he waits for another beauty. A beauty that lasts. He waits for you.

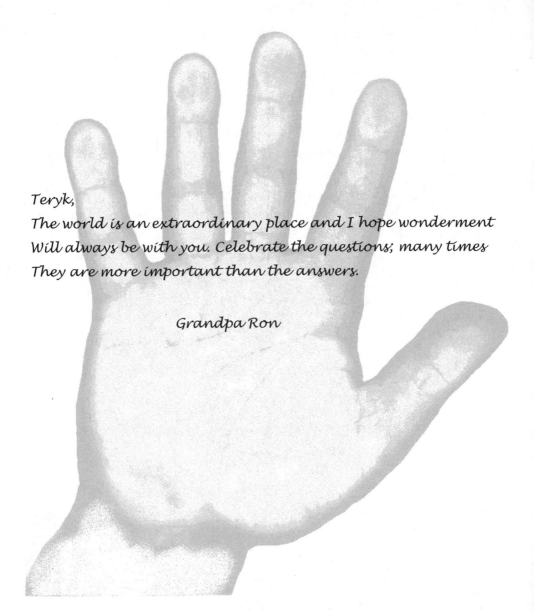

Teryk,
The world is an extraordinary place and I hope wonderment
Will always be with you. Celebrate the questions; many times
They are more important than the answers.

Grandpa Ron

Aunt Davina

February 2, 1998

I walked home from work today and thought about what I should write to
you about my sister, your aunt Davina. As I always do when I remember, I
see what is in my mind and not what I walk through, what is around me.
My surroundings transform into a movie, and I greet myself at five years
old, and I greet my sister at twelve. It is like being in a dream where you
wish you could speak to the ghosts that are now gone, now here but too far
away to speak to though they are close enough to touch.

As I walked, I thought about all of our years together, your aunt
Davina and I, comforted by the knowledge that I would be home at the end
of my walk, that I would take a minute to greet my collection of small movie
monsters and tell them silently about my day. I would open the freezer and
take out a frozen dinner from the top of the neat stack and place it into the
oven, where it would awaken from its suspended animation and fill the small
space of my kitchen with the toothsome aroma of punctual familiarity.
When my dinner was done, exactly thirty minutes later, I would uncover
the uniform compartments with their uniform contents and eat each sec-
tion in order, with the spork I saved from a fast food restaurant. Later, I
would ready my clothes for morning and leave them in a neat pile in the
closet, enjoying the routine. Then I would watch the Andy Griffith show

before reading a little before I fell asleep. The anticipation of these rituals ran as a backdrop beneath my memories of your aunt Davina, and I realized with a deep sadness that these rituals had taken the place of the rituals of my life with her as a child, which I still mourn for. I have ordered my life to map the grief and surrender of my smallness in this world and the certainty we all leave behind when we put our backs to the doors we enter, enter, enter only when we are young. I miss my sister. Sometimes I miss her even when she is standing beside me.

For years, your aunt Davina was the only friend I had, as we lived far out in the forest. I remembered how far away we were as I walked down the neatly paved sidewalk of the city. Davina and I walked the long, wild trails together, in the middle of somewhere, and we swam in the streams and pretended we were explorers, never realizing that we were. But I didn't know her even then.

She was always a very quiet child and always seemed a little sad, like she was born knowing too much and had nothing to say because some old part of her knew it had all been said already. She would sit in the corner and watch, watch and sit. She is an enigma now and her mystery has grown with her, or perhaps it is because she has stayed exactly the same that her mystery is so deep.

If I had a million dollars I wouldn't know what to buy her because it wouldn't give her what she wants, which I suspect is peace in the world; if I were a philosopher queen I wouldn't know what law to offer that would bring her joy. In my dreams I hear her say that she would wish only that everything was the way it is because it can't be any other way, and she would want everything to change. That is where she stays. In between two impossible extremes.

Expecting Teryk

Most people would say that your aunt Davina is tough. She has a black belt in Tae Kwon Do. She wears a leather jacket and rides a tricked-out Harley-Davidson Sportster too fast. She tells people to piss off if they tell her she should wear a helmet or that she should, in the interest of her long-term health, ingest something other than Dr. Pepper and potato chips. To celebrate our family's tradition of going to the Scottish Highland Games each year to immerse ourselves in our heritage, she made her own sword and sheath, wrapping herself in tartan in the old tradition and wearing her sword on her back. Unlike me, Davina is tall and willowy, with long black hair and penetrating green eyes. When a man from the milling crowd at the games whistled at her and called her Xena, Warrior Princess, she coolly walked over to the man, who grew paler with each of her nearing steps, flinching from her green eyes, which were locked onto him with unpleasant determination. She bent over him, her face a few inches from his, and said in a measured tone of grim sincerity, "I . . . am . . . NOT . . . Xena, and . . . I . . . am . . . not . . . a . . . princess." She turned on her heel and walked away with her head held proud. You never really know what is going to set her off.

Your aunt Davina's sense of humor is dry. Once, we were driving her car across the country at night, quietly watching the stars and the fields and the running moon, so comfortable together in our silence that we forgot what silence was. I was driving as she leaned back lazily in the seat next to me. I am what might be called an irritable driver, and when a car in the other lane, the only one we had seen in hours, approached with its lights on bright, I leaped forward to flash the driver. Unfamiliar with her car, I turned on the left turn signal, then the right as I groped furiously for the trigger for the headlights; as the offending car passed us I sprayed the windshield with cleaning fluid and set off the wiper blades for good measure. There was a moment of silence as the wipers squeaked back into position.

"Well. You taught him a thing or two," she said, expressionless.

When I thought about this as I walked home today I laughed out loud, noticing too late that someone was passing me. I saw her face long enough to know that I was doing something unusual, and she looked away from me quickly, quickening her step. I forget to look out for things around me like most people do, or the way that most people do. I stopped laughing and walked on the sidewalk instead of my memories for a moment, but I can't stay that way for long, and I noticed with growing anxiety that I was approaching a place on my walk that I always dreaded—because another way I remember is through context, and if something significant happens to me somewhere I always relive it when I am there again, no matter how many times I return. Today it was worse because I was already thinking about Davina. Like your grandpa she loves to create beauty, but she has little time to do this thing she does so well because like your grandma she loves animals more than anything and spends her days caring for them in an animal hospital.

I thought about my sister as I felt the memory of two years ago start to surround me, punctuated by the cars driving by me too fast and too close. I tried to ignore them. I tried counting my steps to seven and thinking about blue, but the memory came anyway.

Two years ago I was walking this way, thinking the same comforting thoughts about going home and dancing my routine, the same, the same, the same. But an exuberant bark brought me out of my reverie. I snapped into focus and looked for the source of the sound. As my head wheeled with the jolt, I caught a flash of gold across the street. I stopped, smiling for a moment, as an old golden retriever galloped into view. I stood still as the dog stopped also, a smile on its own face. A moment later, a puppy bounded up and stood alongside the older dog, panting and looking around with the bright eyes of wonder that told me that the puppy wasn't used to being out; it had escaped its safety.

A feeling of discomfort started to settle into my mind as I distractedly tried to put the picture before me in context. I felt my smile slide down heavily, in slow motion. I looked around nervously for where the dogs might have come from. I took off my belt and looked for a break in the swiftly passing cars, so I could cross the pavement and leash the puppy to take it home, back to the safety it had burst from to take in the world. Just as I was hoping that at least one of the dogs would have a tag that included an address, the puppy saw me on the opposite side of the street and ran toward me to share his limitless joy, as if he had been waiting to see me all of his life. I saw the car coming.

Time twisted in my chest and around my feet like a clear, hard honey, causing the biting bitterness of fear to fill my mouth as I stumbled forward with agonizing slowness, trying to stop the car that was barreling down the street toward us. I looked back and forth. My head swung first to the driver, who was staring blankly ahead as if nothing before him existed, protected from the outside world by two tons of cold metal that kept him from considering what was to the left of his life, or to the right.

I moved my eyes to the puppy, who was running toward me in stretching bounds, scooping up life in his big paws as he drew them into his chest with each leap and then extended them to hug freedom to his small heart.

I pushed myself into the street.

"NO! NO! NO!" I yelled. I waved my arms. I wasn't sure if I was trying to command the dog to stop or if I was trying to stop time as the inevitable oozed red into a future I knew was going to turn black. I held my breath as the car sped to where I stood, drew parallel, and seemed to stop in my consciousness, as a sharp scream—a sound of submission and apology —pierced the air. A dull, unforgiving thump was the unfeeling reply of a preoccupied street as the car sped on, leaving a pile of gold behind.

I dropped my books where I stood and raced to the motionless form 6 feet away. As I fell to my knees, I noticed the puppy's tail wagging weakly. Only for a flash, I thought the puppy might live as I turned the limp body over to look into the puppy's eyes, thoughtlessly breathing assurances under my breath. *Oh no. Oh no. Oh God. You'll be alright. It's ok. I'm here. You'll be alright.*

When my tight and terrified vision widened and I saw the puppy's whole face, I caught my breath. Thick streams of bright red blood were pouring out of the puppy's nose in the forceful final contractions of his dying heart as his small body struggled and tensed, no longer knowing where its life was. I pulled the puppy into my lap.

The puppy looked at me, panic and pain in his eyes. The puppy looked at me. He looked at me until his thrashing slowed, then ended with a final tensing of his small body as his eyes grew dull. I knew he was gone. I knew the exact moment when his spirit passed beyond my grasp. It was nothing I saw, but something I felt.

The numbness of shock ran ice through my own dull body and I stood unsteadily, cradling the soft, dangling form in my arms as the red streams of what had been life just an instant before dripped from the puppy's mouth and ran down my leg, pooling at the sole of my boot.

I looked to one side and then the other, not knowing how to move, how to think, what to do in the middle of the silence that screamed in my head. Only then did I notice that there were people all around me, silent. All the cars had stopped. I hadn't seen them. Some people were crying.

I cried as I walked home today, and, as before, I didn't realize until they had passed that people had seen my tears and looked away, hurrying past. I am sure that I was an enigma to them.

Perhaps this is why Davina remains an enigma. I think she remembers the way that I do. I think she remembers every animal that has nursed sweet peace from her body as it has passed, and she remembers every sweet, nursing baby, sleeping peacefully that she has cared for. Tears of joy and sadness run like rain in the sidewalks of her mind, where she passes no one.

Tara and I thought about it a long time and chose your aunt Davina to be your godmother. This means that she has made a promise to take care of you at any time that Tara and I can't. This doesn't happen very often, but if it does you will have a family there to take care of you. No one could offer more. She loves. She loves when it bleeds and when it ends, and she loves from the beginning.

Teryk,

    I am your godmother. When Tara and Dawn asked me I knew I'd been given a special gift of a lifetime. Teryk, excited doesn't begin to describe how I feel about you. I'll bug you with all that mushy stuff constantly as you grow up. Right now, I'll just say welcome to your life and to our family. I'll look forward to being a part of your life. I hope it is full of joy and happiness; it most certainly will be filled with love, always.

                Davina

Great-Gramma Eddings

October 13, 1998

Today would have been your Great-Gramma Eddings's birthday.

I have a trailer. It is a 1958 Oasis travel trailer. The oak veneer is perfect and casts a warm glow around the soft, rounded interior. It has all the original yellow Formica counter and tabletops and the original yellow "Princess" stove still works. I named the travel trailer "Bertha," after my gramma, and, as if it were an extension of her ample body in life, it holds the overflow of my many collections, my memories, from the 1950s and '60s: turquoise tea and flour canisters, model cars—Edsels, Plymouths, Chevys—and my collections of B movie aliens, a cupboard stocked with Twinkies, Wonder bread, Wrigley's gum, Velveeta, Jiffy Pop, and Fizzies, which I never eat but open the cupboard to look at sometimes.

On the wall of the trailer is my treasured Spam calendar, along with pictures of old gas stations and motel signs—the kind that incorporate words like "Tiki," "lounge," "comet," and "Flamingo"—and also on the walls are pages torn from old magazines: an advertisement from 1956 showing the perfect turquoise kitchen replete with turquoise appliances, an article on Elvis joining the army, another ad for Ipana toothpaste. In the corner, on some shelves, are stacked pictures of strangers. I haunt the antique store down the road; I pick a box of photographs and sit on the floor with it, going through and, concentrating on each face, picking out a rare picture that speaks to me somehow. Then I bring them home in the pressed safety of your book and place them carefully on the shelf in order that each new arrival can be absorbed into the collection of people never connected.

In the closet I keep some of my gramma's clothes. No one had wanted them when she died, and they were going to throw them away; but I thought of them as an intimate part of her, still smelling of her cedar closet and the Avon perfume she had used since before I was born.

I couldn't understand why people might have wanted her money, her china, her silver tea set, her valuables they called them. I wanted her fingernail file, her false teeth, her clothes. The things she had touched every day.

Sometimes I open the closet and touch the housecoat, the sweater, and the other clothes hanging there. Once, not long ago, I found a tiny piece of used and balled up tissue in the pocket of her favorite blue sweater as it hung in the closet, and I cried for a long time, holding onto the end of the sleeve where her hand should have been.

I'm sitting in my trailer now and it is quiet.

Your Great-Gramma Eddings was what I would say was an older version of one of those princesses in the stories who lead lives of unspeakable anonymity and endless toil until their prince comes to take them away and remind them that they were spectacular all along. But my grandmother lived out that story in turns; from Monday to Saturday she was alone, then, every Sunday, her Prince would come and her prince was Jesus.

I have two rivers of memories about her: first, the short woman who wore the same shapeless dress each day, who didn't bathe during the week because she was fat and felt bad; I remember her smell, one that I guess people would call stink now, but I loved her and that was just how she smelled. She left her teeth out even when she was eating. I remember the woman who was afraid to go outside and waited in her chair by the door for the Jewel Tea man to come and sell her candy and mops, socks and tooth-brushes, bringing the most mundane of the outside world into her dark living room. I remember her lying for hours in the front bedroom watching the birds out the window, coming to feeders that my grandfather had to go out and fill because my gramma was sure that she would die if she went out into the front yard.

But then Sunday morning would come, and the Lord would come out from behind his cloud and banish all that could harm her in the great world and she would transform, and then she would sing for him.

My gramma was in the Sunday choir at the First Christian Church of Carbondale. Looking back, I am guessing that they put her in the front row of the choir because she was four foot eleven, but then I believed that they put her in front because she was best. I believe that this was her conviction also, though she would admit in her private thoughts that pride was a sin in the eyes of the Lord. But then, so was vanity, and she managed to make that another sin that was beautiful.

I would get up early on Sunday mornings after lying in bed, listening to her and my grampa making eggs and bacon and biscuits and tea, my gramma singing her favorite hymns and practicing the ones for this special Sunday, loud over the banging of pots and pans, the spatter of grease in the skillet, and running water.

> *For the beauty of the earth,*
> *For the beauty of the skies,*
> *For the love which from our birth*
> *Over and around us lies,*

Lord of all, to you we raise
This, our song of grateful praise.

For the beauty of each hour,
Of the day and of the night,
Hill and vale and tree and flower,
Sun and moon and stars of light,
Lord of all, to you we raise
This, our song of grateful praise.

For the joy of human love,
Brother, sister, parent, child,
Friends on earth and up above,
Pleasures pure and undefiled,
Lord of all, to you we raise
This, our song of grateful praise.

(Hymn by Francis Pierpont, 1835–1917)

The woman I met on those Sunday mornings was a different woman than the one I knew on Tuesday and Wednesday, as if she was no longer something trapped and smelly in a cage but something free and magnificent. She was proud.

After breakfast she would take a bath, calling my grampa to come and help her get out of the tub when she was done. I would follow her into her bedroom, breathing deeply of the smell of her open cedar closet. I would sit silent on the bed and watch. Still humming songs of praise and redemption she would huff and squeeze into her girdle, stopping to mop the perspira-

Expecting Teryk

tion from her brow as she set her determination to roll on what she referred to as her "garment." I liked to hear her say this word, because it rhymed with "varmint" and I always put the two words together in my mind because her girdle always seemed more like more an untamed animal that she was wrestling, like some saint smiting a winged serpent, than it did a benign piece of clothing.

When she had subdued her garment she would, as she caught her breath, survey herself briefly in the large round mirror of the vanity table she had had since the late '30s. She had grown over the years to fill out the mirror, herself becoming rounder and more reflective, and I used to wonder if people kept their mirrors long enough they would come to look like them instead of the other way around.

Even in the girdle her belly would be round and her chest flat, for she had no breasts. She had had cancer back when the operations took everything. It was a secret my grandmother never talked about, but my mother told me that they had cut away Gramma's breasts and then taken out all the muscles around them and that Gramma couldn't even lift her arms for a long time after the operation. But she would lift her arms as I watched her put on her bra and insert the breast forms she bought through the mail. She would swing her arms around like a little bird learning to fly a second time as she let them settle where they belonged in the two silk nests on her chest. Then she would be satisfied.

She would put a slip on over her bra and girdle and then sit down to do her makeup. I would sit, still silent, still watching, as she put on the layers of color that I always thought matched the notes she hummed and sang as she worked on the face in the mirror like a rare flying thing looking out an open cage door. She would style her hair and set it with clouds of hairspray, misting a temporary halo around her perfect head. Sometimes I would cough, but I always tried not to because if I made a noise she was likely to tell me to go get ready for church and I was always ready before breakfast. So I would sit, breathing through my fingers as perfume followed hairspray. Still in her slip she would slip on a pair of black patent leather shoes and then a dress with a zipper up the back would always come last and she would call in my grampa to help her zip it up because she couldn't reach that far.

I was sometimes bored in church as I sat by my grampa, because people always said a lot of things I already knew, about being good and trying hard, so he gave me little pads of paper made of different colors and a pen from his pocket so that I could draw. I would be jealous that he got to eat communion wafers and drink grape juice from the tiny cups that were passed down man to man to man.

But when my gramma rose up in the wonderful sweep of the dark blue robes that washed the choir up like a storm cloud in God's white sky, I would sit in rapt attention as my grandmother sang like one of the birds that she watched from her window during the long week before Sunday. I was proud.

I always wanted my gramma to be proud of me. The only time I was scared that she wouldn't be was when I told her I was gay. I was sixteen. I put it off as long as I could, then, on Thanksgiving day, I went to find her. She was feeding squirrels outside the front door. She had always tamed the squirrels of the neighborhood and all of them would eat pecans right out of her hand. I sat on the step near her.

"I have something to tell you," I said.

"Yeah?" she said, in that soft, southern way she had, like sorghum molasses looking for candy.

Expecting Teryk

"I'm gay, Gramma," I said. There was a hint of apology in my voice, not because I was sorry that I was who I was, but because I knew she had had a hard life and I didn't want it to be any harder. I'm sure there was the sound of fear there, too. She had a choir singer's ear and I wondered if she heard it.

She cracked another pecan and the squirrel, hearing none of what I had said, took it from her, sitting calmly as his world stayed just the same. She was quiet for so long that I thought she might never speak to me again. I felt like dying.

Finally, without looking at me, she said, "I had a friend like that once." Another timeless pause. "A long time ago." She was looking into the distance now, at a past I couldn't see. I still wonder what she saw in the distance, just beyond me.

"Yep. I did. She met a nice man, though. Got married, even loved him because he was a good man. They had kids." I thought she might be holding this story up as an example for me to follow. But she went on.

"She always wondered, though, what her life would have been like if she had lived it some other way." Finally, she looked at me. She didn't have to say anything else and we never talked about it again.

I sit here in the silence of my trailer, and I wonder what it would sound like if my gramma sang in here. It would be too loud unless she sang softly, like she did while she was looking in the mirror. I go to the closet and open it, taking the empty end of the sleeve of my gramma's sweater in my hand. There is a small mirror on the inside of the closet door. I look into it and sing. It is quiet.

Great-Grampa Eddings

March 7, 1998

When I think of babies conceived in this time of the spring, I think of my mother's father, my grampa, your Great-Grampa Eddings, who was born on Christmas Eve and started to grow in late March nine months earlier. I would like to think that you will be conceived on the same day that he was, but time is secret about those things where my grampa is concerned, and so I will be content to dream it.

My grampa used to like to tell me the story of how he came to the town I grew up in. He didn't know the part about his grandfather's grandfather's grandfather coming from the ancient Celtic lands where our family so long had lived, leaving for Virginia, generations running through South Carolina, through Tennessee, through Kentucky, so he left that part of the story unspoken. I would find it later. My grandfather told me only about his history, the personal kind that he thought was his alone until he was old enough to see it belonged to everyone.

He came from somewhere south, riding in the back of a pickup truck, the wind of the first decades of the last century at his back and in his face; his face square and kind, as if it had recognized and accepted the weighted pressures of the world from above, below, and each side.

He told me that he was filled with happiness as they crossed the city limits, though what he might have been happy to leave behind or happy to look for in our town he never revealed.

He said that as they passed the sign marking the town, he took his watch in his hand and threw it as far as he could out into the fields, singing dizzily past the truck, and he said goodbye to all the time that had gone before. I know from my memories that he got another pocket watch, but he rarely looked at it, and time meant something different to him. Like the watch he had thrown from the truck as a boy, time from then on had lain in the fields for him, and it was never two o'clock or nine o'clock, but time to plant cucumbers or time to plant pumpkins or time to can okra pickles. For your great-grampa, time was something that strung invisible between the harvest moon and the silent poems of catfish; it was a pool like old, and a garden rain like new, time was a smell like when it was right to take biscuits out of the oven and a taste like knowing it was springtime.

I remember watching him digging in the garden once, when I was six. There was a warm wind blowing, and though it paused, it did not stop; I knew that this was the voice from the ground my grandfather was opening, and I also knew to listen, because the ground speaks only once. My grampa wiped his moist forehead with his pocket handkerchief and kept digging in earnest with his old shovel, his heart and mind involved in the activity of lifting small loads of dirt to let them go behind and away.

I felt like sitting and watching and so I did. I wasn't in a hurry. There was nowhere to be. And so I sat and watched.

"That looks like hard work," I said.

"Yes . . . ," my grampa said in a bare whisper, wiping his forehead on a sweaty arm and smiling, "it is."

"What are you doing?" I felt easy, letting the external world give my tangled inner voices hush as I let the fresh earth beneath us contain me. It was a peaceful and unusual feeling.

My grampa leaned on the shovel and looked up at me, and I didn't look away.

"I'm aplantin' tamatas." There was a gravelling, shucking sound as my grampa hard-scrabbled the shovel into the dirt, displacing sleeping dirt and glancing off unseeing rocks—between the sounds of the biting tool was the sound of the stones and dust whisked over an invisible shoulder into an invisible wind.

> The eyes of the stones
> Look out on the sea,
> Past the horizon
> Where stones used to be.
>
> As long and unblinking
> As the gaze of their hearts,
> The stones of dreams' islands
> See the dawn of the dark.
>
> And with a stone memory
> As old as stone sight
> They dream of the winds
> At the edge of the night.

The repetition of the digging was familiar. Anything repeated looked familiar. I needed the predictability of doing the same thing—anything—over

Expecting Teryk

and over again, sweetly anticipating the surety of an act in infinite parts, all feeling the same; I loved the stability of thinking ahead to the thing that was happening now, and now, and now, knowing it would feel the same in a few seconds as it did in the moment, like fingering a rosary of acts in a chaotic world in which God only shouted and forgot. I watched my grampa dig and plant, dig and plant, counting the beads of his mind and body, saying prayers that peace had come to earth at last.

As far as I knew, my grampa had been here since all these things first came into time and would last until they were all forgotten, just like his love for my gramma, whom he met at a church dance and fell in love with at first sight. He didn't need to spend time with her like most people think of ordinary time, because he came to her with a soul as old as the dark before the Lord stepped up to my grampa's side and thought about light. And so they slept, in the dark, side by side, on the many nights I slept within the shelter of their old house.

Sometimes when I was a child I had nightmares in the middle of the night, nightmares of things old . . . things hairy . . . things made of memory. I would wake, sitting up in the dark, unsure where I was, my heart pounding and my head salty, until a car, and then perhaps another, would pass on the street. Then, as I gulped and shook, their headlights would sweep into my consciousness and offer a three-second dream of the daylight. My mind would shimmer up around me as the quick brightness brought a glimpse of the familiar, only to disappear just as quickly and allow the dangerous edge of black to swallow me again, engulfed in darkness and cut with the light of vision and voice, quickly extinguished. If I tried hard I could move slowly, but only if I keened lowly—as if my muscles were attached to my voice and the pain itself was telling me to move and stay very still, black as if an ink was swirling up my body, invading my mouth, my nostrils, my eyes, my ears. With agonizing slowness I would make my way down the hall to where my grampa slept beside my gramma. As I would tiptoe through their doorway I could see the clock on the stand next to my grampa. The clock's face glinted, standing guard resolutely around the hands reaching out from the small, square cog in the center, unmoving; it wouldn't keep time here, where he was, inside the outside of myself. I blinked in the blackness and listened for the sound of his closed eyes, waiting for the sweeping light of his soft sleeping to bring me out of the dark singularity of my confusion. A flash of white cotton light soaked the ink from my eyes and ears as I felt him, felt his love call to me even from his dreams, and then I would go back to bed.

On the table next to my own bed was a child's wind-up clock with a sun, a moon, and stars and a window on its turning face. The window crept along, showing what people should be doing when it was nine, when it was three, when it was seven. The numbers around the outside were pushed from importance as the picture kept my attention. What time was it?

The window would show you. I would wind the clock and listen to its song as I fell asleep.

Aaannnddd ttthhheee ccclllloooccckkk
ssstttoooppppppeeeddd
nnneeevvveeerrr tttooo rrruuunnn aaagggggaaaiiinnn
wwwhhheeennn ttthhheee ooolllllddd
mmmaaannn
dddiiieeeddd . . .

He would have loved you.

PART 7

Getting Pregnant

Your First Name

February 24, 1998

I have always been interested in beginnings. Not only in the big beginnings, like where the universe started and where we all came from, but small beginnings like what comes between 0 and 1 and the ways your little spirit is taking shape. Though as I said, no one can be sure where anything or anyone starts, we can see small sparks—"there . . . ," we say, "and there . . . and there . . . "—when something happens that helps to make a thing begin and grow. Your name is just such a spark, a trying and growing in the vastness of space that speaks to me of one of a million places you begin and end.

My interest in beginnings invisible and apprehended, both small and large, helped me to find names for you. It was a special task, because your name will sum up all the beginnings and endings in your life, from the first time we will say it to you and welcome you into our arms. We will call it when night is creeping in around the warm to cool of summer nights when it is time for you to come in from playing. Your friends will speak it as you become a part of their families in a way you will never have friends again. Your love will say it to you in the dark, and later, if you choose a life like the one I live now, your own child will say it with the breaths of the first part of her or his life. Your name will live longer than you do and will be spoken when you yourself are a living ghost on your family's faces as they turn into the future.

When I was in school learning about where our human ancestors came from I became interested in the stories that people tell, stories from all over the world, about the ghosts of our ancestors. Everywhere people tell stories of the people who lived on the land before them. The stories always tell of hairy people with big teeth and flat noses, brown skin and heavy brows, people who travel over the lands secretly with their rough tools and a way with plants and animals: a magical people that can still be seen in dreams, a magical people that speak to the living. My favorite story of the wildman is from eastern Europe. I found there a story of the Teryk —literally Dawn Man. Wild people are the First People. It is in the stories. They leave a brown trail.

In the stories, the wildman is a great teller of stories, though his messages are often cryptic: not from an obtuseness born of deliberate obscurity; rather, they are undeciphered in the same way that messages from one's own subconscious can be cryptic.

Wildmen and wildwomen are revealed in accounts of the "Golden Age" passed down to us from Juvenal, who tells us that "during Saturn's reign, when a cold cavern provided the humble home and hearth . . . wild woman (the Lare, the spirit of deceased relatives) unrolled her wild bed of leaves, straw, and animal skins. . . . Then, in a new world, under a young sky, men . . . lived in a different way."

The earliest literary example of the wildman is Enkidu in the Epic of Gilgamesh found in Old Babylonian and Sumerian texts. The original writings, which are written examples of earlier spoken stories, are dated as old as the

Ur III period (ca. twenty-first century BC). Enkidu was created from the clay and was "shaggy with hair" over his whole body. Gilgamesh scholars believe that the epic was based on an account of the creation and early life of humankind. In Edenic descriptions it was said, "With the gazelles he feeds on grass, with the wild beasts he jostles at the watering-place." Enkidu knew nothing of civilization and was ignorant of bread and wine. He freely associated with the animals and the land and was inextricable from nature and his natural state.

In both Hebrew and Arabic folklore, Adam, the first man, had a tail like a monkey until the Lord eventually "took pity on his dignity" and removed it, whereupon he used the raw material to create the first woman. Talmudic commentary on the fifth book of Genesis includes a requirement that those encountering an actual ape recite the benediction "Praised be he who changes what he has created."

In South America, indigenous Guianans, Venezuelans, Brazilians, and Surinamese talk about the wildman; they call him "didi" and "didi-aguiri." These wildmen build crude shelters of palm leaves, and, if large parties of humans penetrate their areas, they group together to throw sticks and mud at them.

One of the most interesting accounts of the wildman of the Tierra del Fuegians came from none other than Charles Darwin, the Father of Evolution, in chapter 10 of *A Naturalist's Voyage Round the World:* "[the Fuegian] also related that his brother, one day whilst returning to pick up some dead birds which he had left on the coast, observed some feathers blown by the wind . . . he peeped over the cliff and saw 'wild man' picking his birds . . . he found the place like the form of a hare."

I wonder if this image influenced Darwin's ideas of our early human lives.

The wildman has always served as an ancestral image. The Yaqui of Central America tell us that wildmen are "departed ancestors" and have the ability to induce dream states. They live in families where wild mothers and wild children have close bonds and wildmen keep the families together.

There are interesting carvings of the wildman from the Columbia River area in Oregon. They were first seen by outsiders in 1877, when O. C. Marsh was allowed to view them and then stole them from their original stewards. According to Marsh, these precontact stone heads looked so archaic that their similarity to living apes immediately suggested itself. Is this possible? In the end it doesn't matter. It is the mystery that clouds and makes beautiful.

People tell stories of the wildman, stories that turn toward the deeper truth of him rather than the science. I like these stories not because they are real, but because they are like you, full of potential and possibility—full of a mystery that science has nothing to do with.

The wildman, called "boqs" by the Bella Coola Indians of the northwest coast of Canada and Alaska, is described as being completely covered in hair, as having long, swinging arms that reach below its knees and a broad and powerful chest, and as being shorter than the average man. One story, related by John Green, tells of a Bella Coola man named Qaktlis and his family, who were camping near a place long associated with the boqs when they heard the creatures in the forest behind them. The man and grabbed his gun and, frightened, told the wild people to go away. Instead, the wild people got closer and began to loudly break branches and beat on tree trunks as they came nearer and nearer. The man grew so frightened that he fired his gun. There were roars, grunts, and pounding in the forest, and the breaking of branches continued. The family could hear the boqs as they rushed around, only the vague outlines of their forms moving like ghosts in the darkness.

Another Bella Coolan story, from the same chroniclers, involves people in a canoe, who came around a promontory to surprise a boqs collecting shellfish. Upon seeing the people, the wildman quickly picked up some clams and ran away, only to return a short while later. The people entertained the idea of shooting at the boqs, but its supernatural power was so great that the man's gun exploded in his hands. The boqs called loudly and at once more wild people came running to him out of the forest.

Lauren Green relates that among the indigenous peoples of Canada and Greenland the wildman is called the "toonijuk." The toonijuk are believed by the Inuit to be representative of an ancient tribe that inhabited the land and hunting grounds before modern people. Though very similar to humans, the toonijuk were hairy and had long arms. When one Inuit was asked when the toonijuk lived, he replied, "Long ago, before my grandfather was born," and to an Inuit, that means "beyond memory."

In ancient folktales from China and Japan the Wild-Beast King has long, thick locks of hair and his body is covered with them. He is very strong, and a single blow of his huge fist can break large rocks into pieces. There are written Chinese records telling stories about the wildman that are four thousand years old.

In the Hawaiian Islands people told fantastic stories of the wild people. The Menehunes were a race of small people that were stout and muscular. Their bodies were hairy, their noses were short, and their foreheads protruded over their eyes. They fashioned shelters from banana leaves in the mountains. They learned to carry stones and shape them. The Menehunes were known by the elders, who, though they had never seen them, said that the wild people came from a distant time and possessed great spiritual powers.

Aldo Massola, who writes about the legends of the Aboriginals, tells us in *Bunjil's Cave: Myths, Legends and Superstitions of the Aborigines of South-East Australia* that the wildmen spoken of by the people are called Net-Nets and Ngarangs. They are human in shape and size but have hairy bodies. They are said to live among the roots of gum trees or make their homes in caves of rock. The great wild people are held in very high regard and afforded a great deal of respect. They come from another time, the people say, beyond the dreamtime, the first people.

In Africa, the birthplace of our own end, the Mbuti call the wildman Muhalu. The Muhalu is exceptionally large, walks upright, and is covered with dark fur on its body and white fur on its face. The Muhalu physically and psychologically overwhelms anyone who experiences it. The Sehite of the Ivory Coast possess a full coat of long, red hair over their human forms and are said by indigenous people to be seen only once in a lifetime, and the observer must be alone in the forest.

Perhaps the most popular image of the wildman, familiar to our culture through titillating television shows and hastily written books good for the young, good for their secrets on long summer nights, is the "Yeti" of southern Asia. Long a part of the culture, the Yeti continues to live in Tibetan religious art, appearing in *thankas,* or painted wall hangings. Yetis are portrayed in the cosmic scheme as beings who are intermediate between humans and other animals. Sometimes the Yeti is the offspring of a human girl and a gorilla.

Expecting Teryk

In India there is a sad story of the wild Ban Mancche—one that reminds me of the sorrowful ending of all things old. In the story, a man from the village of Sijaburha had gone hunting in the forest. The man spotted a wild boar at the same time that a Ban Mancche had also spotted it. Before the man could aim his gun, the Ban Mancche, who was also hunting, threw a stone and killed the animal that they both stalked. The Ban Mancche ran to the dead animal and at once cut its chest open and took out its heart. The old Ban Mancche looked at the heart very carefully, just as a man would do to see the future. He then knew the truth of what was to be. The Ban Mancche felt his end near. Rather than be killed by another, the Ban Mancche struck a powerful blow at his own head. The next moment, the man shot him. He was already dead.

People tell these stories because there is a memory in them that is more real than things that walk in our sight, that reflect light and invite touch. It is important to us that the ghost of wild people live just beyond sight, breathing in the air of the ancient forests as we breathe all around them, unseen.

Alone in the forests of my mind and heart I have seen my wildman. He is you, my son, the small, wild thing to whom I tell these stories as if I will see you only one time.

Dawn man. Your name reminds me of not only the larger beginnings of our people but of what my mother told me about my own name. She said that she and my father had thought of me as the dawn of a new life for them and so gave me that name. You will be the dawn of a new life for me, but you will also be the dawn of the future and a continuation of our past, a dawn of time stretching back to the first people and walking ever forward to the dawns only our children will see.

Your Second Name

Your second name, like your first, is very special. It comes from the Gaelic language of our ancestors nearer in time. It is made of three words:

bryd = heart

anial = wild

un = one

All together it means "heart of the wild one." This name came to you in honor of the best friend I ever had, who was a silverback gorilla man who lived in the zoo. When I was in school I went to the zoo to learn about gorillas and how they did things because they have kept many of the old ways of ancient people and have a lot to teach us about how people lived a long time ago. But I learned much more than that from the gorillas. I learned how other people feel, I learned about humor and sharing, and I learned about talking without words.

For much of my life I couldn't stand to be close to anyone. I longed for it, in an oblique way, at an angle that no one could see. I was like those wild children I've read about whom no one remembers seeing before they emerged from the woods, bits of stick and moss in their souls. The books say now that these children were probably autistic and had either been left in the woods by parents perhaps more merciful than it would seem, or maybe, they say, the children couldn't take the human world and ran away.

My friend Congo, a five-hundred-pound silverback gorilla man, taught me how to be loved and not run away, how to look into someone's eyes without collapsing, how to sit with someone quietly without the need to count. He was gentle and loving, though he had had a hard life, like me. He taught me to love.

He didn't see that I was impaired, or poor, or different. For so long I had needed a man in my life—not to romance me or make me feel complete—but to add to me somehow, to protect me, to allow me to love him. I think because it was comfortable for me as a gay woman to be around women all the time I never realized that there are other ways to need a man's spirit in my life. Congo reminded me of the best of my grandfather, the best and rare of my father, the brother I never had, and the son I started to long for. He was large enough in body and love to remind me and inspire in me all these things.

Congo died on February 27, 1996. The human people at the zoo wanted to know what made him sick and what made him die so that they could help to save other gorillas in the future. They sent different parts of his body around the country so that they could be opened up and studied, so, they said, people could understand what had happened to him. I want other gorillas to live and be well, but part of me wanted to take his body back to Africa where he had been born, to thank him for a life given for us.

The hardest day for me was when they sent his heart away. I couldn't stand the thought of Congo's love going away.

After awhile, I understood that his love was everywhere, in me, and in people who love me. I realized that when we take in our last breaths, reversing our first loud inhale with a quiet exhale, when our naked bodies shake, slick with sweat in place of that first wetness when we come into the world, when we have been delivered through that tight, black hole that marks the end of floating at the end of a cord and signals the beginning of our freedom, we are reborn. The new ghosts will celebrate you Teryk Brydanialun: the man of the dawn, the heart of the wild one.

Who Will Carry You?

March 3, 1998

As I write this I think about the wildest women. Among the coastal tribes of the place we live they tell stories of the wild woman who serves as a teacher for all who would be mothers. She is called the "dzonakwa," and she lives in caves, the people's stories say, laying in stores of meat, berries, and fish, providing for her family. She is a strong woman. A womanly woman. It is by her power only that a girl can become a good mother. In his book *The Way of the Masks,* Claude Levi-Strauss, the well-known anthropologist, tells us that among the southern Kwakiutl Indians, pubescent girls actually ritually become the dsonakwa in preparation for motherhood and the regeneration of the people. The girls wear a costume consisting of woven goat's hair so that they can look like the wild, hairy woman and sit immobile in a private shelter for a month; they are allowed to eat only some salmon and sip water through a bone. Maybe this brings out the wildness and strength that is already within them—the cunning and ferocity to protect and provide, to need and to nurture.

Though I know I have strength and ferocity to love and nurture, the only time I have ever felt consciously like a woman, a singular sex, was when I felt pregnant with you. I remember that feeling well, though it lasted only a fleeting glimpse. The memory of that time brings home to me how different I must feel from other people, who seem conscious of being a specific sex every moment of the day, seem to need to feed that feeling.

I have always felt that I was a woman and a man, or more truly every woman and every man. I try to find the boundaries that make me just one person and I simply can't find them. I think a lot of people have assumed that I have felt that way because I have always been a lesbian; many people in this culture have strong opinions about gayness and gender going together. If you are a woman who likes women you must think you are a man. If you are a man who likes men then you must think you are a woman. But I don't think that's true. At least, that hasn't been my experience.

I always pictured having a family but never really pictured giving birth. Tara thinks she would enjoy being pregnant, and we both like the idea of me taking care of her while we go through the pregnancy that way. Your mother has always been a very "womanly" woman. I am sad to say that our culture often forgets what this really means and thinks that to be womanly one must look somewhat artificial, dress a certain way that may not be very comfortable, and talk a certain way that makes her appear less strong. But I think women who are naturally womanly, or feminine, are nurturing and protective, strong and yielding. Of course, men have these things within them, too. But women have a different feel, a different flavor. Perhaps it is indescribable; I don't really understand it myself. I am not a man or a woman, but really more like a brain on stilts.

Maybe the way I feel like neither, or both, or nothing, is because I am autistic. I feel like the environment I live in and my body are the same thing. Though my way of seeing and experiencing the world is a wonderful thing,

Expecting Teryk

it is sometimes very uncomfortable. Whether the way that I am has its center in my body or my spirit, or both, almost everyone in my family is like me, and for some of them this way of being has been more pain than beauty. I wouldn't wish that for you.

Anyway, we both know that Tara would make a good mother. When she was younger, Tara used to see babies and want you so bad she would cry real tears. I know that when she thinks about you, her arms ached to hold you and she cries about it sometimes when we see new mothers out in the world, their tiny babies' inch-wide fists flailing pinkly in the air. I hug Tara and tell her you will be here before we know it. I can't claim that I understand her feelings, and sometimes I sigh heavily over her shoulder and wonder what in the world is in her bloodstream that wasn't in mine (mostly hormones, I think). You will be lucky to swim in her.

I have been giving a lot of thought to my body and how I fit in it. I have almost never had any regrets about not having a real body; I have been happy to never feel alone in some nebulous sense. But I find that right now, as Tara and I think about bringing you into the world, I have been struck forcefully with the regret that I can't make you in the usual way men and women do. It started as a vague thought in the middle of the night and then grew until it held me in chains, taking my breath.

I read once about a man who had had polio as a child and felt so self-conscious about his withered leg that he hid his body all the time and would never let anyone touch him or make love with him. As I think about ways to make you start to grow, I suddenly feel unwhole for the first time, pierced with the realization that there is a withered and invisible part of me that never even existed that will never be there.

I went for a walk with a friend the other day. We strode over the hills under our trail in the woods and then silently climbed a lookout tower above the bay, the puffing of our labored breaths the only sound. As we paused to take in the wide view, he caught his breath and smiled at me. He told me that he and his wife were going to try to have another baby, a planned one this time, no accident. I told him I was happy for him, and I was. I understand now why that kind of news makes people happy.

His smile changed to a grin I couldn't decipher. Then he said that he imagined that having sex to consciously make a baby must be the most exciting experience anyone could ever have. I said that I guessed that could be true. What do I know?

It bothers me now, for the first time, that I won't ever know that exact feeling. I wouldn't choose it even if I could, because I could never want something to be that kind of bodily part of me. I'd be too afraid to do that to a living thing.

As we descended the stairs of the tower I felt myself sink deeper into my sadness. It was as if suddenly I had gotten a glimpse from a different tower, looking out over a certain barrenness of my own land. It felt like an important limb of me had failed to grow, or had not been given to me by the generations gone before. This is where it ends.

As I write this I think of those generations. They have given me everything. They wouldn't have forgotten something so important.

A Dream about You

I had a dream last night that you were here. You and me and my whole family, even your Great-Grampa Eddings and Great-Gramma Eddings were there. We were all sitting on an old fashioned screened-in porch at the end of a hot summer's day. You were naked, a beautiful blonde little boy with your grampa's blue eyes. You were running up to people and jumping in their laps, laughing, laughing, though the dream was the kind with no sound, the kind that moves slower than life.

I woke up and told Tara that I dreamed we were going to have a little boy with a wonderful smile, who loved everyone and whom everyone loved.

How Will We Get Pregnant?

March 21, 1998

As I sit at the table and write this morning, I carefully arrange my three breakfast Twinkies in a perfect triangle on the plate I always use in the morning. I put down my pen to make a final adjustment to a Twinkie that is slightly out of alignment. There. Poetry.

I always feel a wave of calm wash over me when I contemplate their symmetry. Perfection is so simple when it comes down to it, really: spongy golden cylinders filled with perfect white cream arranged simply on a predictable surface. I have always loved this kind of balance, this kind of order. When I was a child I would arrange all my many collections in my room, just so, looking at them from all angles and making minor adjustments for as long as it took to reach Perfection. When each rock, each stuffed animal, each saved bottle was in its divinely ordained spot in the universe I would sit still in the middle of my bed and sigh with bliss. Why should life be any more complex than that? I will never understand why it is.

But I have to face the fact that it is. Take sperm, for instance.

Sperm helps an egg grow into a baby. Sperm is something that men make in their bodies and in families where there is a man and a woman who want to be a father and a mother it is (usually) simple for them to

make a baby. When you have two women who want to be mothers together, they usually have plenty of eggs but no sperm in sight—so near and
yet so far, as the saying goes.

Tara and I thought about asking someone already in our family, or a
friend. But most people love children, and when they help make them they
understandably want to be a part of their lives. Many of the men we thought
of asking to help you grow would have wanted to be with you all the time;
who could blame them? But Tara and I want to be your only parents.

People have found themselves in this kind of situation for a long time,
but the mechanics of the solution remained obscure. A hundred years earlier, in Italy, the physiologist Lazzaro Spallanzani discovered that sperm
played a vital role in conception. Then, exactly one hundred years before I
was born, Gregor Mendel, a monk from Austria, discovered the basic work-
ings of heredity—the blending of two separate cells from an ancestral line.

Artificial insemination was first practiced in the late nineteenth century, but it was a very secretive thing. In 1949 people invented a way to
freeze sperm for later use. At first people used this technique only with animals, and the fact that commercial air travel became possible at about the
same time changed the way cows had babies forever; soon after, it changed
the way humans could have babies also. In the 1950s it became common to
conceive this way—after 1953, when the first human born from frozen sperm
squalled into the great breath of the universe. It is odd to reflect on the fact
that because of the invention of frozen sperm, your genetic father could
have been dead for years by the time you were conceived.

I remember being very interested when, many years ago now, some
people had discovered the mummified body of a five-thousand-year-old
man in the melting glaciers of the Italian Alps. In one report I read, re-

Expecting Teryk

searchers, who had by then moved the body into controlled cold storage, received countless inquiries from women who were hopeful that the Ice Man's sperm had been frozen with him, as they were interested in bearing his children; a kind of virgin birth heralded by a Stone Age God, holding his axe and bow, his face pressed into and kissing the blessed and fecund earth for thousands of years, waiting for the annunciation.

I wondered if the reality of the clinic and artificial insemination was the poor relation of the Virgin Birth, as Tara and I had our first visit to the fertility specialist earlier today. It was hard to believe that life could start in a place so white and free of dirt; I always think of life being a thing that starts in the loam and tear of the mossy dank, and if you were a seed, your growing would happen as easy as a peach seed growing a tree after it falls on the hot, wet ground, part of a sacred grove.

There was a studied absence of the spiritual in the clinic. We were there to stick to the facts, to understand the science in that surface way that science is meant to be understood. We were told that we would need to choose sperm from a catalog that the clinic provided, that we would get an ultrasound on a certain day of Tara's cycle—I listened absently to the recitation of cycles, four days, twenty-eight days, forty days. Tara would get an injection to ensure her ovulation within twenty-four hours, and then we would have the selected sperm introduced into her uterus, near the fallopian tube, the day after that. I wish it were as uncomplicated as putting Twinkies in a triangle. Oh, well.

The words rang off the bare walls of the clinic, and I found that my feelings of growing and reaching and planting could find nowhere to hang and burrow in. It was a barren place.

Amid these thoughts I assured myself that many children were indeed conceived inside these walls. Perhaps none of them would, by themselves, resemble the product of the Virgin Birth I thought about, but each would be holy when the parents who loved them left the cold trials of the forty days and forty nights of the clinic and carried their children to green and growing places. But the clinic was cold.

As I sit here looking at my Twinkies in the warmth of the kitchen, I think about the cold that a part of you is frozen in. Some vital part of you is suspended in time and space as I write, in the dark of a stasis chamber hundreds of miles away.

It was cold in the Klondike exactly a hundred years ago, exactly a hundred years before your conception, when people left their old lives behind, striking into new territory to seek the gold of the Klondike gold rush. There was plenty for everyone, it was said, and they tried to beat time and get it all for themselves. I think of my grandfather throwing his gold watch, gold in the field, for no one, given away for a new life, a way to stop time in a new territory.

As Tara and I paid for the beginning of your new life and left the clinic for our new lives, we sent out gold for the few and the many, and the one. We have thrown the watch into the field. We have paid for time to stop and start again, in new territory.

Your Sperm Donor

March 23, 1998

I watched a show on television once that told the story of a family whose son was saved when a stranger donated a kidney to him, to replace his own, which were very sick. The boy would have died without the new kidney, and so this stranger, this man, gave him life. The family eventually met the man who gave their son his kidney and told him what a wondrous thing it was that he had given a part of himself so that their son could live. It is the mark of a loving person to give in ways that she or he may never see the results of, to help people he or she may never know.

Like anyone who donates a part of themselves, like blood or organs or sperm, the man who donated sperm to help our family grow must be a person who cares about other people's happiness and wants his community to be happy and healthy. Your donor gave a part of himself, knowing that it would go out to help start a new life that he might never know, trusting that we would take care of you and protect you. Though we don't know him and he doesn't know us, perhaps we will meet him someday. One thing I know for certain is that he must wonder about you.

We know a little about him from the sperm bank because the people there told me many things about him to help me decide who would be the best person to choose to help you grow. Tara and I decided that I would choose the sperm donor myself because the man giving us sperm to help you grow would be doing my part; he would be representing who I am and parts of myself that I would help to add to you as you grow.

To help me make this decision they sent me a catalog to look through of men who had donated. The catalog helped me to make some beginning decisions. Every person who chooses sperm from a bank has different things that are important to her and that help to guide her choices. For me, it was important to find someone who shared my ancestral heritage because that is still an important part of who I am. So I looked down the list and saw a few entries that caught my attention:

Ethnic Origin	Hair Color	Eyes	Height	Skin Tone	Occupation
English, Irish	Blonde	Blue	6'0"	Medium	Humanities
English, Welsh	Brown	Hazel	6'2"	Medium	Biophysics
Irish, English	Blonde	Brown	6'4"	Fair	English Literature
English, Scottish	Brown	Blue	5'9"	Medium	Oceanic Engineer

Once I had selected several candidates from the catalog, I sent off for what the cryobank calls "short profiles." These are a packet of a few pages wherein the donor describes himself, what he does, what his health history is, and what he thinks in response to some basic questions like what

Expecting Teryk

his favorite foods are, what his favorite color is, what his favorite animal is, how he would describe his personality, and what his ultimate goals are in life.

I was so excited when the four profiles came in the mail, and I immediately sat down on the couch to read them over. I was discouraged indeed as I went through the first three. One of the potential donors, when asked what his favorite animal was, said he didn't like any animals at all. I don't think that genes are everything, but that struck me as potentially pathological, and I literally threw that profile over my shoulder and said goodbye to it before it hit the floor.

In another profile, the man said that his sole ambition in life was to make money and that he would do it at any emotional cost. The man in the third profile conveyed in the personality portion of the questions that he was, in fact, "perfect." Since I was looking for someone to represent me, I had to throw that one out, too.

Then, as I looked at the last profile, my heart leaped with joy as I saw untidy handwriting—looking uncannily like my own, all in capital letters —scrawled unselfconsciously into the margin as the donor's blooming thoughts ran beautiful riot in the margins of the sheets. He spoke two languages fluently (he had spent part of his young life in another country) and two more on a working level. As hobbies he ran a business, did film and art, and wanted to go to too many places to list (one of them was space, where I'd be happy to join him). His favorite color wasn't just an ordinary color, but a specific color on a specific fish's back; he was a careful watcher of the world. He was eccentric by his own admission and very, very intelligent, loving to pursue knowledge. Like me, he liked to write. His ultimate goals were fantastical, and I admired them. As a bonus, the last two digits of his birth year were two of my favorite numbers (though this would obviously not have been a deal breaker). It was like looking at a form that I myself had filled out; I knew that he was the right man.

For fun, I sent my photo into the cryobank to have them match my appearance with the donor's on a scale of one to seven. They rated our similarities a five.

The Day

March 25, 1998

I got up at three o'clock this morning because I was too excited to sleep. We had the ultrasound yesterday, showing us exactly where the egg that is going to make you is growing; it showed up as a small black hole, like a deep and secret cave where things learn to see without eyes and follow invisible currents downstream, led by dreams of light. We couldn't see the actual egg—it's too small—but we knew it was there, waiting.

I watched the sun come up, clearing a bigger darkness. I am too small for it to see, but I believe that it knows that I am here, like a waiting egg. It is the dawn of my new life.

We drove to the clinic, holding hands in the car for a while because we had gotten there too early. We sat and looked at each other. Sometimes we smiled, sometimes we looked down at our linked hands, scared.

When we went in they led us back to one of the gleaming white rooms, and it reminded me of the hospital where I was born. Tara lay down on the table, on a deerskin I had brought, and she held a pouch with some of my grandparent's hair, some of Congo's hair, and some other objects we hoped would bring us luck, like some plant fossils I had found in a stream when I was very little.

The doctor came in with the nurse, who showed us the mighty tea-spoon's worth of pink in the oddly curved syringe as she held it up to the light. You were in there swimming around, I thought, one of 10 million sperm; simultaneously you were waiting in the dark of your mother, two places at once.

I took some pictures with a camera I had brought, so we could look at it years from now and see the exact moment when the two parts of you started the last part of their journey to meet, so small a distance and yet so far, after the many travels of an egg that was inside your mother already when she was born and 10 million sperm that had made two trips across the country, suspended in the air, suspended in liquid nitrogen.

Our appointment was at noon, and the doctor placed the sperm about three inches from the egg. He told us it would take about three hours for the sperm to travel that final distance. During those three hours Tara and I were close to each other; we went to have veggie burgers at our favorite restaurant, we came home to be next to each other. We sent good wishes to you, floating in wet darkness, free of the new and sterile, claimed once again by the oldest things.

It is 6:45 p.m. as I write this. You are alive.

PART 9

Growing

Knowing

April 1, 1998

A few days ago, when you were yourself only a few days old, Tara told me excitedly that her breasts were aching and tingling. She said that she already knew she was pregnant. It amazed me that she knew already, and then again it didn't. For though as she spoke you were a hundred cells, you are so real to us and so dear.

By now you are a rolling raspberry of cells, falling off the dark but loving brink of your mother's womb, falling, again like a ripe raspberry, into the warm ground of her sacred places, becoming covered by her living soil. At this stage you are what they call a blastocyst, which means "sprout pouch."

Because of the way my mind works, the way it affects my hearing, I can't hear words without forming images that are sometimes deep and solemn, like the brown of memory and trail, but sometimes funny, like when I hear "sprout pouch." Though I know you have no human body yet, I see you as a tiny version of the Jolly Green Giant with one small, green-slippered foot stuck like an anchor in the side of Tara's uterus, one small hand holding a bag of green beans. Sprout pouch. It's a neurological thing.

95

In reality this small pouch will grow bigger, filling with amniotic fluid to make you your own hidden ocean, and you will grow the way that wild, green things do—in silence, under the heat of a deeper sun.

Today is April Fools' Day. It is the wildman's day. Deep within the traditions of our people we see him, the Green Man of this time of year, reminding us that the universe is a foolish place full of delight one can drown in.

He comes to us in stories from the lands of our ancestors and tells us that when he is the "Phynnodderee" or "Hairy-One" on the Isle of Man he is a spirit fallen from grace for dancing in the glen, but that he is very kind and helps gather hay and carries quarried stones cross-country by night so that the people can make their stone houses. He tells us that in the Scottish Highlands he is the hairy brownie tied with ancient family lineages, he who throws clods of dirt at passersby to protect them while his wildwoman kin assures that the family will never go hungry unless they forget the ties that bind them to the wildfolk and turn away from them.

And in Ireland he tells us that the hero and the holy are insane. In ancient Gaelic traditions to become wild expresses a kind of rite of passage that is necessary to attain purity and/or priestliness. Forget what you know. Forget what you know.

It is folly to believe that we know much of anything, and if we clear our minds we see the man of savage brown and green bounding over the hills, laughing. He has sprung from the earth, his own sprout pouch, growing.

I imagine you, my wild son, floating in that great internal sea, bumping over the fertile internal hills of your first home, the first home of our ancestors, the first home of the Green Man, seas of rain in the Great Isles.

I read once that of all the human organs that fall apart and return to the earth after death, the uterus is the one that lasts the longest, holding its shape, waiting. I think about the land of old and salty water that you are in now and wonder if ghosts wear death preservers when they go swimming in wet and secret places because water is such a life-instilling force.

I think of this as I slip quietly into the bathroom in the morning to watch Tara shower. I sit nearby on the floor and watch her graceful movements under the cascade and think about water running over her and through her, nesting in the dark of her still-flat stomach, like an inland sea.

When I touch her (and I seem to need to touch her all the time now), her skin is softer, and she smells different—sweet and warm. I don't want to be away from her, and a dull longing starts in my chest when we part to go out into the demands of our days. Though I have been inside her in a hundred ways, I now wish on the stars in her eyes that I could stay somewhere among her folds as I feel panic rising within me.

I reflect on my panic, on where it comes from. People have tried to tell me it is part of my "condition." I agree with them, but my condition isn't the same thing that they are thinking of. It comes from being a wild animal in this culture, a person who cares about the wild things around her and sees that they are slipping away even as they come softly. I hear the wild spirits call my name in words, and I wonder where they come from. I close my eyes. Pan, the wildman, is playing his flute.

The word panic is derived from his name, I remember. My memory comes back even more behind the pounding of my heart. I am turning his stories over in my racing mind.

Vladimir Markotic, in "The Great Greek God Pan," says that in stories of old, Pan's appearance and yell could cause confusion and shock as he communicated in strange voices to one raw of heart, wandering in the forest, and also that he appeared in dreams in order to reveal the future.

In the earliest Greek depictions, from the fifth century, BC, Pan is portrayed as hair-covered, with a pug nose, and carrying a *jagobodon,* or hunting stick. He was unusual among the gods in that he lived alone in a cave in the mountains or forest. The first being to live, he was born even before Zeus, but unlike the other Gods, he was mortal. Pan was a protector of wild animals, fishermen, beekeepers, and hunters, being himself an excellent hunter.

I feel Pan hunting me now. Though he has ever stalked my delirious dreams and slain my peace, a god of my past, he now becomes my fear for the future. I think of my tiny, wild son, the growing wildman, the Dawn Man. You have put so many nightmares to rest, and now you have created new ones.

Tara steps out of the shower, like a clean Aphrodite from a shining shell, an opposite. Her beauty, her body, stills my fears and grows them, Pan behind her eyes and within her belly. Over and over I count to 3 and try to let the fear make words. Pan tells me the future.

Will you love me? Will you like me? Will I be a good parent? Can I protect you? Can I protect your mother? 1. 2. 3. What if something happens to Tara? And you—you are in the silent dark. If you needed me, would I know? If you died, could I live? 1. 2. 3.

I imagine an ancient ancestor counting, counting, like saying spells, laying out stones in threes and calling the numbers in a long-forgotten tongue. The Green Man, the wildman, Pan, making us both holy, making us both Fools, both insane.

Just as in his world the green never dies and the uterus is the last of the body to return to earth, I return from the edge of fear and let hope grow in its place. I put a trembling hand on Tara's middle and pray.

The Green Man's wild has bent its head under a sheltering blanket; it sleeps while I can't and lets me greet the first hidden sun of the day. We had a late snow last night, and as I write a soft white down of cold flakes lies on the ground and mirrors the sky, not knowing whether to be blue, or gray, or white.

I took some food out for the birds, a little seed, a little peanut butter. It seems like they take turns at it, their tiny bodies, lighter than snow, changing places in a world where they worry about each other; nature pale in tooth and claw.

The birds remind me that we are too quick to judge what we see and hear sometimes. Perhaps it is not a matter of survival, or fitness to live, fitness to reproduce. Perhaps it is about the struggle itself and the way that triumph—or even living—is a shared property, a way the living know each other.

I was touched by the story of Kidogo, a member of a captive community of bonobos. Kidogo had a serious heart condition and lack stamina and self-confidence. Commands from a keeper thoroughly confused him, and in his need his friends—including the most dominant of the bonobo men—would calm him and then guide him, taking him by the hand, to gently lead him in the right direction.

In another group, this one of Macaque monkeys, a monkey named Azalea had motor defects and was slow to develop socially. Though monkey society is highly structured and competitive, Azalea was accepted by the other monkeys; she was not peripheralized or attacked by the others she depended on.

My favorite story, however, is of Mozu the snow monkey. Many of Japan's native macaque monkeys are born with awful deformities of limb believed to be the result of toxic agricultural chemicals. The mutations include added fingers, clenched fingers, missing fingers, and missing hands and feet.

Mozu was such a monkey. Born in the spring of 1971, she lived in the Shiga Highlands of Japan, in a community that lived farther north than any other known primates in the world. In the harsh winter snows, deep and unending, Mozu would scuff through the drifts on her elbows and knees, for she had no hands or feet. Though her mother helped her when she was young, when Mozu was older she was determined to do for herself. The other monkeys would climb trees, which made their way easier, but Mozu could not climb and had to crawl fast to keep up with the others, who welcomed her presence among them as they made their way down into the valley to eat each day.

When Mozu was seven she gave birth to her daughter Momiji. To keep her daughter safe as she rode on her chest, Mozu walked with her limbs extended as far as they would go. This constant effort was exhausting to her, but she kept up. In the fall, when fruits and nuts came, the community moved quickly to eat as much as they could; Mozu had to eat what she could find and scurry quickly along to build up her fat reserves for the winter. When snow fell, Mozu was forced to eat the toughest bark and twigs near the ground because she couldn't climb up into the trees to reach the more tender growth, which the other monkeys enjoyed easily. Carrying a baby through the snow was grueling work, but Mozu held on.

She had a son, and then another. Two years after that, Mozu had another daughter. Still later, an aging Mozu had another son. All of them were healthy and had no deformities.

Growing

Mozu was an excellent mother and rose above her challenges to raise a perfect family. Soon surrounded by her children and grandchildren, Mozu was the picture of a successful matriarch.

In Japanese Shinto religion, monkeys are believed to be the messengers of the gods and to commune with spirits in stones. With a will and love like the mountain spirit and rock, Mozu stood as a member of her people and started a new generation. I take her as a testament to what I can become.

Over the past two weeks I have been thinking a lot of Mozu, how different she was, and how despite her differences she was included in her community. Perhaps it makes no difference that her disabilities were not traditional, that they were the result of a recent poisoning as unnatural, as some would say, as orange grass.

I can't think about Mozu and difference, or primates and evolution, for very long without turning my mind to my own unnatural differences, for so they are called by some. Like orange grass and green sky, my kind of difference is natural in small doses.

I have been reading *Biological Exuberance,* a book by Bruce Bagemihl. In the book, he illuminates homosexual behavior in animals from dolphins to hummingbirds, from macaques to marsupials, from bats to buffalo, asserting in the introduction that the book, which is 751 pages long, is woefully incomplete. The book could have been more concise perhaps, but for the wonderfully inclusive fact that the author recognizes that actual sexual contact is but one part of a vast repertoire of same-sex behavior; he rightly includes courtship, affection, sex, pair-bonding and parenting.

In his research (compiled from many sources) Bagemihl has found that many birds, such as lesser scaup ducks and sage grouse, have within their communities lesbian pairs that raise offspring together. Bonded female pairs of grizzly bears, red foxes, warthogs, and dwarf cavies, each with their own children, will nurse each other's.

In other species an individual female without young of her own will bond with a female with offspring, helping her parent and protect them: such is the case with squirrel monkeys, northern elephant seals, and jackdaws.

Growing

Pairs of male Rheas will incubate egg clutches and raise young together. Male black swan couples will associate temporarily with a female, and once her eggs are laid the couple chases her away and broods the nest and raises the cygnets as their own.

Still other species' same-sex pairs will adopt offspring that are not biologically their own. For instance, two northern elephant seals occasionally adopt an orphaned pup and raise it together, and pairs of male hooded warblers and black-hooded gulls may adopt eggs or entire nests that have been abandoned by females. Pairs of male cheetahs will sometimes take in lost cubs.

Bagemihl goes on to show that successful same-sex parents have been documented in at least twenty species and in some cases have been shown to have certain advantages over heterosexual pairs—especially in species where single parenting is the norm or in situations where two males can defend a larger or more desirable territory.

In terms of our own primate evolution, Bagemihl, citing Paul L. Vasey, estimates that the blossoming of homosexual behavior in our very early ancestors occurred during the Oligocene Epoch—24–37 million years ago; this estimate is based on the distribution and characteristics of homosexual behavior among contemporary primates. With all those years of practice, higher primates have become very expressive and creative in their expression of homosexuality.

Forms of pair-bonding such as consortship, favorite partners, sexual friendships, and even exclusive or preferential homosexuality are found in chimpanzees, pygmy chimpanzees, gorillas, and other primates. In spending time with my own gorilla family I saw females who liked to hug each other, mount each other, and generally share each other's company when one was in estrus, or her mating period. I even knew of one gorilla female who might have been considered transgendered had she been a human being: her shoulders were very broad (much broader than other females'), the hair on her back was the silver color associated with adult gorilla males, and her behavior was distinctly "unfeminine" for a gorilla of her supposed sex. Her assertiveness and reluctance to back down in situations where other gorilla females would have readily acquiesced brought her trouble time and time again. She often sought out the affection and sexual favors of the only other adult female in the group.

As I turned the pages of *Biological Exuberance,* I was interested to learn that other female gorillas had been seen to form pair bonds, constantly touching each other, sitting with each other, lying against one another. These females will have sex with each other, caressing, engaging in oral pleasuring, and making love face to face (this last is notable as normally during heterosexual sex, gorilla partners use a rear-mounting position).

Male gorillas also seek each other out for sex and affection, and gorilla males are as likely to be mounted as they are to mount. Older, higher ranking males will actually guard younger males they are bonded to. It is known that female apes are capable of orgasms both in heterosexual encounters and with each other, and so are males; observers have seen evidence that males have reached orgasm together.

In "A Speculative Consideration of Certain Possible Forms of Sexual Selection in Man," published in 1959, George Hutchinson suggested that there may be evolutionary value in homosexuality. Because homosexuality appears to be an evolutionary constant that occurs at a rate that excludes the possibility of it being a "mistake," he reasoned, it must have a useful function and further, it must have some genetic basis. Other researchers, such as Edward O. Wilson and Stephen Jay Gould, added their voices to Hutchinson's, suggesting that homosexual individuals may fulfill the role of "community helper," aiding their compatriots in a number of ways, specifically in the nurturing and adoption of children.

I remembered hearing about this very thing happening in a group of chimpanzees in Jane Goodall's study. A certain grown female chimpanzee had always had female consorts—had defended and protected them in fact. She had spent her leisure time patrolling with males and had generally acted like a male chimp. She had never had children of her own. Eventually she adopted several orphans and became a wonderful mother. I think about her and the gorillas I have read about who love each other. I am so close to them—genetically, or in experience, perhaps.

I am in good company.

April 20, 1998

We got up at dawn this morning. We went into the bathroom, and Tara sat down, waiting for me to open the box we had been waiting to use since before you started growing. I read the directions and handed her the little cup to pee in. She blinked sleepily and stood. I placed a few drops onto the test strip while we barely dared to breathe. I could feel Tara's early morning warmth as she bent over and rested on my back, peeking over my shoulder, looking for the purple line that would match the purple line of the horizon outside our window, signaling a new day. Like the sun coming up over the hills, the aubergine glow started faintly, almost a trick of the eyes to one who stands looking back at the long night, then rising, unmistakable. It was there.

What started out as a single cell has now divided into millions, and you have already begun to differentiate within your tiny body. Some cells go to making your skin, your nervous system, and hair. Others go to your circulatory, urinary-genital, and musculoskeletal systems. Still others go into forming your gastrointestinal tract.

At four weeks your arms will appear, looking like buds at first. Your heart will divide into tiny chambers. Small pits will mark where your eyes and ears will be. Brain lobes and a spinal cord will develop, along with all your major organs: esophagus, trachea, stomach, mouth, liver, gall bladder, and thyroid. At five weeks you will have paddle-like hands. More than a million cells are added to your body each minute.

Still, you are so tiny, a whole world. I think about how important so small a cluster of cells can become; in so many ways, you will become my

Growing

world also, and I think of you, the size of a poppy seed, like an unseen planet in a minute and private universe, one that I inhabit with my mind, within my own cells.

Your heart started beating today.

Dear Teryk,

Although you don't know it yet, this is my first Mother's Day with you, and your first with me. Right now you are tiny, just half an inch long, but I can feel your presence.

In my belly is a firm spot that already makes it hard to bend forward or wear my pants. Now and then I feel my womb shift, as if it's adjusting for you. I've been tired and queasy for the last few weeks and I realize that my symptoms remind me of your presence; if I'm lucky, you will be in my life for the rest of my life. Dawn and I are so excited to feel you grow—we can't wait to meet you. Sleep well my little one; I'll take good care of you.

I love you. Tara

You have started to have detectable brain activity, like all babies at your stage of development. Your brain cells reach out and touch each other, forming neurons, making pathways like fingerprints as you start to mesh the parts of you that were smelted in the internal explosions of hot stars millennia ago with the new internal explosions of your waking ability to perceive. A hundred thousand new nerve cells are being created in your brain every minute; in the time it took me to think about this and write it, you have created five hundred thousand nerve cells.

Your hands and fingers, looking like paddles and sprouts, wave and blossom like the waiting buds and veined leaves of the green wildman in a rain-soaked garden, and I wonder if someone who reads palms could look into the minute creases and swells there and tell your future, your fortune. Perhaps if they were to look, they would see only the short future, the kind they might read in the palms of small animals, and perhaps that is the only kind of future that babies have; maybe the future written in your spread fist tells only of the untold wealth of having a life, the inevitability of your birth, of a new hand.

Does this make you real? I try to release the question out loud, outside of myself as I look out on a world of shadows, never knowing if the shadows are caused by my own inner explosions—my thoughts and hopes—or if there really are things that exist through a reality of their own. There is no easy answer, and I close my mouth, my silence real to me.

The nature of reality and the forms that exist within it, whether shadowy or material, has been a difficult question since before I was born and you were conceived. One point of view is that all we perceive is the result of combinations of matter in motion, ultimately fixed and unchanging. Another extreme is the notion of an immaterial universe, in which all we can perceive is ideas—there is no substance to the world.

A middle paradigm between materialism and immaterialism, perhaps even between the dark inner world you inhabit now and the one I see as I write, claims that all knowledge that is universally communicable has two components: it must have content available to our senses and there must be mental structures to organize and interpret that content. The synthesis of these components results in knowledge, or what is real.

When we relate our experiences about what is real to someone who holds the same experiences and archetypes within themselves—as we all do—experiences take on additional life. They become more real. To me, they become alive.

The distinctions people (who consider themselves both real and living) usually make between what is real and not real, what is living or not living, do not resonate with me.

The real and living seem to believe that in order to be real, something must be perceived by them. The jump and run of a cat or the swerve of a snake does not make a thing real. A thing must be seen or smelled or heard within the narrow range of our seeing, our smelling, our hearing, to be real. The jump and swerve of people makes things real.

And to be alive, a thing must move within a certain range of speed. If they can't measure it moving, then it isn't alive; too slow, like rocks, and a thing has no soul, they say, or if a thing moves to fast, like light. Sometimes it seems like people can't accept the idea of living in a living world. It scares them to death.

But paintings are alive. The sky is alive. Rocks are alive. I've seen them born and I've seen them die.

I remain a ghost, though, feeling as unborn as you are. Sometimes people seem to share this experience of me and make it more real. They look through me as if I wasn't there, look right through me as I lurk around, making funny movements and speaking gibberish, haunting the places where people go, with a hollow hungry look. *Where is my history?* I wonder, as I feel an older one than other people talk about. With this question I keep my history—my own and my family's, both mine and not mine.

Your great-great-grammy Prince was a keeper of history that way. She took pictures of every moment from our first sunny days to our Big Passages: births, deaths, funerals. Around her house were piled photo albums and scrapbooks that commanded obeisance, like a monk's library where light coughing rings out like Satan's curses.

She was fond of Will Rogers's saying—that the only news is the history you don't know, and you were expected to sit quietly, listening and not touching, when she blew the dust off of a heavy register of lives past and still looking and cracked it open to show you the future.

She worked in the hospital where your aunt Davina was born and sneaked into the nursery to take her picture as she waved her chubby fists in the air, even though it broke the rules. "It was for a good reason," she said. She had a long history of breaking rules for good reasons and knew where the line was. It was somewhere inside her, a bright but invisible divide behind her eyes.

She married a foreigner, a rich French man, at a time when such things could be seen as scandalous. She never said much about it, or other earlier

Expecting Teryk

wild things I suspect she had done at the turn of the last century, but they were as clear as a book of pictures and sat on her lap when she rocked on her stone front porch and primly swilled beer from a can, unapologetic.

When she heard that I had married a woman, she knew that I had broken the rules for the right reasons, too. She sent me a card.

I am so glad to hear the news. It is hard to find someone to love in this world, and when you do, hang on to them. It doesn't matter what anyone says, what matters is that you are happy.
Sending you all my love,
Grammy Prince

My happiness was real to her.

Her son, my father's father, had different ideas about what was real. It may have been because he was a young man when he had children, but then, so was my father, and my happiness was real to him in a way that his own was not real to your great-grampa. His name was Earl Prince, an unnecessary royal redundancy, looking back. Perhaps it was because he knew such plenty that need was not real to him. My father's mother told me once that she thought she might have gotten pregnant with my father behind the counter of the Prince Cleaners, located in the Prince Hotel, where she worked because she was poor and where my father's father didn't because he was not. She was sixteen. I saw her once, in one of Grammy Prince's books, a child holding a smaller one. Earl wasn't in the picture. He had left.

I wonder if he used to think about his history. Grammy Prince never seemed to pin it down in any of her family books, and I think it was lost. He drank as unapologetically as she did, but where she, once again, knew where to draw the line, he did not. He died years before she did, and I know

now that she must have felt her own history fall into dust, as all mothers do when they must keep the books they intended to leave.

She died last week, while we were pregnant with you. She was old and tired and she died in her sleep, sleeping the way that you do now and seeping into endless dreams where she can live it all over again. I imagine you passing each other in the dark. She waves her long and wrinkled fingers. You wave your hand, a paddle with buds. When you are born I will send a picture to her old address.

Rebirth

Here, alone in the mid-day sun
I move, I play,
I jump, I run,

I feel my muscles move in time,
beneath my skin,
my body rhymes,

I have known how to move
to eat
for so long
in such a quiet way

that it is a joy to move like a child
when I am no longer hungry.

I am reborn.

Often, late at night, I stay up, alone in the dark, and watch old monster movies. I have been recording them for years, and, like so many other things that soothe me, I have an enormous collection of them. At last count I had about two hundred of the old classics (and many obscure, bad B movies) and enough aliens saved from celluloid to tape to take over any galaxy of my choosing.

Some people have tried to analyze my attachment to these movies, and all of what I have heard them say is true. I like being immersed in a simpler time—black-and-white movies with black-and-white plots. I need the predictability of the scripts because I really, really don't like change or the unexpected. Some have said that I also like the predictability of the triumph of good over evil, but this is where their analytical skills fail, at least in part.

It is true that I like knowing what is going to happen at the end, but my small secret, like a secret that is not terrible but quiet in its own simplicity, is that I always root for the monster.

While I am at times antisocial enough to wish I was the last person on earth, I don't wish people harm—even the fake kind of harm that comes from Death Rays or Evaporator Beams, or the realer kind that comes from being knocked feet away by a long, menacing arm. I am not against humanity in this case, but rather for the monster. I have always been one myself. When the movies continue to have the same endings, the same deaths large and small, I sometimes pick up a monster from the neat row against the window and apologize to it, holding it tenderly, as if it were a smaller version of myself. My monsters look back at me blankly, unable to speak.

I have always lived in a separate universe, trying, at times, to visit earth's inhabitants and failing miserably at my task. Like Klaatu in *The Day the Earth Stood Still*, I leave the armored walls that transport me across space and time, the walls that let me sleep in a vacuum, and make my thoughts reach out with a wave of my hand, only to extend the invitation of my companionship and be fired at because I can't make myself understood. It isn't anyone's fault. It is always frightening for both sides, each monstrous to the other.

I roll it over in my mind. I think about the origins of the word monster. It comes from *monstrare*, which means "to show" and from which we derive the word demonstrate. The monsters show us something important.

Tonight I watched my favorite movie, one that has become an archetype for me. It is Jean Cocteau's version of *Beauty and the Beast*, made when film was young and the listening human heart still had an ear for story, story such as is told around the fire or when little children go to bed.

In the movie, a poor father goes on a journey to try to obtain money to keep his family together, to feed them and put a roof over their heads. Before he leaves, he asks each of his three daughters what they wish him to bring back. Two of the daughters want expensive and beautiless gifts, but the youngest daughter, Beauty herself named, asks for a single rose.

Caught in a storm without finding any fortune, the father is led by the soul of the forest itself to a magnificent and hidden mansion where he sees no one but where his every need is tended to. Disembodied hands light his way with candles and pour his wine at table. Statues whose eyes follow him keep silent vigil as he sleeps. As he is leaving to come home the next morning, he pauses in the garden to pluck a single rose to gift to Beauty.

The beast, whose mansion has offered succor to the father, appears in fury and demands the father's own life for killing the rose.

The father begs to deliver his gift and then return to die. The beast grants him this request, and the father returns home to tell the story and bid farewell forever. Unselfishly, Beauty rides out in the morning to take his place.

She is kept captive at the castle, where instead of killing her the beast finds his heart in her and tries tenderly to win her love. He is hideous to her at first. Hair covers his body, and his fangs, like fearsome fire, cut from his mouth. Like most monsters, his raw maleness whispers of a barely restrained power, a power over life and death. A creature of immense sensitivity, he is helpless under her touch; when she delicately places her hand on his, then strokes the hair of his body, he begs her to love him.

Eventually, Beauty does come to love him. In other versions I have seen, the focus is on the end of the movie, when Beauty's love transforms the beast into a normal man, completing her happiness. But in this version Beauty falls in love with the creature as she watches his animalness; she is aroused when she watches him lapping water from a stream, sensually offering to let him drink from her own trembling hands, tenderness welling within her as he dips his tongue into her palms—an exculpation of savor. She is deeply moved when he returns bloody from his hunt, his hand bloody and smoking. In this story she is clearly saddened when the beast loses his monstrosity and becomes an ordinary man.

Tara and I had an ultrasound. It was exciting to see your strong and fearless heart beating, your hunched and curled body hiding in its own mansion in the heart of the growing wild. Tara cried with love when she saw your face.

You are a boy. Your teeth are forming and you will soon have twenty tooth buds hidden beneath your gums, waiting to erupt in a fearsome fire. You have grown a fine and delicate hair all over your body, over your very thin skin. You can respond to touch now, but though your tongue and vocal cords are just forming, you make no sound—a censor of absence. You are monstrous.

To me, this is beauty.

July 22, 1998

As I think of you evolving, my thoughts naturally turn to the evolution of the human family. Through my choices I have blended the history of the new with the history of the old, and I realize that all that is old becomes new again when we heed the call of persistent things—like death and birth.

As I write I give you a history that already belongs to you as you hang suspended in the dark. I give you a history of myself, of your family, of your family's family, who came over the oceans, and of their families, who came over the land, over the land, from places on the other side of the world and on the other side of time. Time itself is dark, and in it is suspended history itself—history conceived and yet unborn.

If you look back, far back, as you hang in dark time waiting to be born, you can see the family of humanity waiting to born. Perhaps they are waiting still, but waiting or born there is a part of the story that science tells. It is the story of where we came from. They tell it like a tree with branches and roots, a tree full of shrews and monkeys and apes. In their story you are the bud waiting to burst from the dark at the end of the branch.

The old primates that would be our ancestors' ancestors split off into a group and made a branch of the tree we sat in during the Oligocene over 23.3 million years ago. The Miocene epoch began about 23.5 million years ago, followed by the Pliocene, which started a recent 5 million years ago. Our ancestors split off from the ancestors of the living primates after that, and we and other primates went our separate—but in many ways parallel —ways until this day.

I love to think about our ancestors' names. To me, the names are the same color as the brown word trail, perhaps because both they and their names are trails without end, a place where we can trot after our tails, everything soon turning the same shade of dun, becoming one thing. *Proconsul africanus* thrived from 23 to 14 million years ago in Africa, its wide face looking out on its sunny days from beneath its hanging brow ridges, its body as small as a modern Rhesus monkey's. *Pliopithecus* left Africa for other lands to the north during an early animal migration 16.8 million years ago, while *Sivapithecus* emerged from Africa 15 to 14 million years ago, when the land there became dry and the forests bid it farewell and embraced the running grasslands. Looking like a chimpanzee, it walked away with its back to the south, calling softly behind heavy teeth, looking for trees.

From Africa our ancestors moved out to live in the places our family wouldn't leave for millions of years: *Ramapithecus* in Turkey 16.5 million years ago; 15-million-year-old *Sivapithecus alpani*; *Ankarapithecus meteai*, 11 million years old, found northwest of Ankara. *Sivapithecus sivalensis* in China, 8 million years ago. They traveled with wide faces turned toward the new, setting their powerful jaws, moving ever closer to the dawn and dusk on huge hands and feet. In my memory's eye I see the largest primates ever known living in Asia during this time: *Gigantopithecus blacki* and *Gigantopithecus bilaspurensis*, both twice the size of the gorillas I have known. And others, *Ramapithecines, Dryopithecines*, moving into Hungary, into Germany, everywhere over the lands that saw us.

As these rough people came north, Europe was becoming seasonal and temperate. The evergreen forests were replaced by open woodland that eventually formed a belt along all of southern Eurasia. From 15 to 12 million years ago, the more seasonally adapted biome and its open country environments extended over central and western Europe, north and east Africa, the Arabian Peninsula, the eastern Mediterranean, and west and central Asia. I see them as people, walking with their arms stretched up to the leaves, looking for each other. Seeing them this way is a mirror for us as a wild people, wild people who make up a family, doing what families do.

The long childhoods our ancestors may have had gave them time to learn to navigate in their cultures: to understand social rules, to make things like tools and to build shelters, and to become good parents when their turns came. Because these skills were learned, not instinctual, they took a long time to learn, and to pass on.

Some scientists surmise that the common ancestor of apes and humans would have to have had, even as far back as the mid-Miocene, an immense memory store, highly developed reasoning ability, and highly developed learning ability to exist in the mixed habitat it adapted to. They imagine that this ancestor constructed shelters from readily available vegetation or by scooping out holes or caves in the dirt that probably had overhead cover as well. These nests or shelters would have been built in clusters that reflected our ancestors' social orientation and would have served as fixed points to which food and tools were brought back. These elements of family and home must have been with us through the dark of time.

As we move forward in time, we find more material evidence, evidence that has left its own footprints—literally and figuratively. Found when a group of archaeologists in Tanzania were playing football with dried elephant dung, the "Laetoli footprints" are trail made by our ancestors, Australopithecines, almost 4 million years ago. They are preserved in volcanic ash and represent three individuals' fossilized tracks, conjectured to be those of a leading male perhaps followed by a smaller female and an even smaller offspring.

Expecting Teryk

The strongest fossil evidence that early hominid families were bonded to each other comes from these prints. In a paper on the hominid footprints from Laetoli, L. Robbins infers that it was the largest of the three, perhaps a protective male, that walked first, followed by the individual of modern female human size, who carefully stepped into the footprints left by the leading member, holding the hand of the child walking beside her.

Of course, there are other ways to interpret the prints. Perhaps it was a grown son who walked first, his mother or younger siblings behind him, or a large woman followed by a smaller woman and her child, or a mother followed by two children, an older one helping a younger one along. Perhaps it was a larger man followed by a smaller man and a child they had adopted, its parents killed by the eruption of the volcano that blew ash over their steps. Regardless of these combinations, one thing is clear.

They were a family.

June 23, 1998

It is raining. I walk along the trail I take each day, making prints that I know will disappear. I think about the Laetoli prints and how some prints will never fade, prints that are already so deep and so invisible that the rain of sky or tear can't reach them. They are inside us, these prints and these people. I think about walking beside them, the Laetoli people, as if we were not separated by time and space. In so many ways, and with such certainty, I know that we are not separated and that they walk beside me now, inside me; through their eyes I see the world; the skin of their feet lifts me on the earth, and their beating hearts make me love, make me care. It is their kind of care we feel when we love and act, when we love the child and the stranger, even the child who is a stranger to our blood.

I heard a story about a baby rhino who was stuck in the mud, and I sing it through my head as the mud under my feet gives away the memory of the dirt.

The baby rhino called and called from the place it was trapped. Its mother came but didn't seem to think anything was wrong, for she left. The baby called again. An elephant came to help the baby rhino, using her tusks to try to raise it gently out of the mud, prying under the rhino's small body, lifting. As the baby struggled, the mother rhino came back and chased the elephant away. When the mother left, the elephant came back and tried again to free the baby, spending hours, dodging the charges of the mother rhino. Eventually the baby freed itself. Perhaps it couldn't have done so without help.

There is evidence that the two larger people who made the Laetoli prints may have been taking care of the child together for reasons beyond family attachment. R. H. Tuttle reveals that the prints of the child appear to have an asymmetry in foot angles that suggests great injury. It is possible that the child had suffered a fracture of the femur (the long bone in the thigh), femoral fractures that healed improperly, slippage at the head of the femur, or maybe a fracture of the tibia in the lower leg. Such an injury would clearly render a child in need of help securing food and shelter and perhaps of medicine, as well as a slower travel pace. So it seems that the ancient child's companions may have been walking slowly and near the child they had given life to or saved as if it were their own, in order to protect the child from predators that might notice its weakness and see it as alone. Mother love is within all of us. I have it for you, my son, and for you stronger than any, but I have had it for others—others as distant from my blood and so connected to my soul. It is an animal thing.

I think about a different trail from the one I am walking on with my feet. I think about the trail of mother love, so old, so old, as I continue to think about all of the different kinds of families and mothers there are. My footfalls match the rhythm of my heartbeats as I walk this trail, this love given from some archaic place, given from the weak to the strong, given from the poor to the rich, from the imprisoned to the free, from the unlikely to the unlikely.

Some years ago a three-year-old boy fell into the gorilla enclosure of the Brookfield Zoo. He fell twenty-four feet from a wall that marked the boundaries of a world the gorillas would never pass through, from a sky that belonged to others outside the circle above their heads. He fell into the gorillas' cell, their cloister, in a few seconds leaving behind the civilized world of those who capture and entering the world of those who release, the world of the wild ones. Everyone feared that the boy would be killed as a gorilla mother, her own infant on her back, approached his unconscious figure. But she picked him up tenderly and cradled him, then carried him to a side door of her world, helping him back into his own world, a world her own children would never know. That is the song of mother love.

I hear it in the birds singing around me, telling the young things of the world to come and fly. For them the sky belongs to everyone.

I read once of a naturalist who gave a chicken mother some duck eggs to nurture. He assumed that the chicken mother would be stupid and treat the ducklings like chicks. When the eggs hatched, the mother chicken immediately walked down her own trail, leading the ducklings to the water and encouraged them to swim. She would never have done this with chicks of her own body. As a mother she knew what her duck children needed.

Another story that I read made me sad. In an experiment humans separated rat mothers from their babies, putting the babies at the far end of an electrified grid so the humans could watch what the rats would do. The frantic rat mothers, who wanted to protect their children, always crossed the grid, over and over, to bring their children back to be near them. The mothers were shocked all the way across the grid, both when they went and when they came back in later experiments. One rat mother made the two-way trip fifty-eight times to rescue all of the babies that needed her. The experiment ended when the scientists ran out of babies.

I believe, as I make tracks behind me and in front of me, that no one knows how old mother love can be, that the blood that ties us is outside of ourselves, the family of life was in the beginning.

As the year truly warms I take the dogs out to run through the fields, to run among the trees, to run to the ocean. Each day a sticky heat calls us down to the cleansing and forgiving waters to lay our feet and our daydreams in its cooling wash. An ambling amnesia, I think, amniotic. I take your book with me, and often I write poems about the places our soft feet fall and the things we see, the things I think about.

In the field, mayflies and dragonflies huzz. I hear the grass as we stalk by: *shush, shush*. It is telling us to be quiet. The spiders are hunting.

I stop and look. In a floating flet, pulling and yarding streams of sweeping shadow, soft flows of shimmering shadow, the webs are everywhere. Everywhere the whispers of soporific spinning, an inhumation of essence, the winding shroud.

In the whisked web in the wind, ossuaries of the legged living are hung in beatific limbo, in incandescent sleep. If I look closer, I can see the tiny eyes of the spinnan, the spiders of the old language, speaking the old language still; still they are, still they are. All of the spinnan pose in pregnant pause, ignoring the desiccated husks about them. The husks and spinnan both waited in the same way, seeing only the motion of the air.

Was there any difference between a chrysalis and the silent, shrouded embryos of the forgotten? Maybe they are both revenants. I think about mercy. Perhaps spiders are kind.

We know now that they think. Under the heavy and waiting eyes of entomologists, spiders have been put through mazes wrought with the walls of human ingenuity, tests woven with the silk of skepticism, in which they must make novel choices, puzzling things out, thinking small spider thoughts. They anticipate. They succeed. They stretch beyond themselves, like tailors making thread inside themselves.

I read a story not long ago by a child whose mother was autistic. Of course, the child didn't know it then. This mother was a tailor. She couldn't drive, she couldn't cook, couldn't touch. But she sewed and sewed with beauty and soul, sliding and needling perfectly, making perfect things. This child who wrote about her mother the tailor loved this beauty of winding and plucking; behind the words were an image of the child and mother sewn together through the countless stitches of unspoken words, shared heartbeats. There was a web of memory, of groceries bought, a tidy, warm house, a mother who protected her children with an easy venom. A kind of quiet, threading spider.

I look at the spiders' webs and ways under the sun, wondering what they want. An insect buzzes, oblivious, caught in nothing. It wants to go forward but struggles, perhaps confused. The sky has never stopped it before. A spider races down like legged lightning and bites. It races back to its corner to wait. I watch the struggling insect, slowing, slowing, mirroring the motionlessness of the spider. They are already becoming one thing. I think of spiders thinking small spider thoughts, stretching beyond themselves. I believe they have mercy.

I see that they run fast, breaking their prayer as they run to the prey, knowing its fear and wanting to stop it. I believe they think about the speed of kindness, their delicious prickle of draughts of sleep and the tight tickle of embrace. They run away, back to their corners, because they know they are frightening, and they wait for the day dreams of dragonflies to become night wakes, sleepy, singing insects in repaired webs, like Celtic Grave Sleepers, hearing the voices of those who went before as they lie among those who have already passed.

In a spinning wind in the twining twigs,
There is a waiting wall,
A place of lacement between the stems,
Swaying, a hazy maze, a holy cross,

The dream of a waiting plait,
A racing tracery,
A piece of splice
In the gentle breeze,

An ebbing web,
An intangible entanglement,
The intricate catch with no knot,
And a spill of killing,

Where wrapping happened,
Spun home in home spun,
Caressing the carcass,
Leaving an architecture of artifact,

A purse of mercy.

We build things with wood and stone and nails, and in our souls we hope to approach the perfection of the web while we fear being eaten by a quick-moving God. We move around the earth and the earth moves around the sun. The web is round.

The dogs run ahead of me as I near the shade of the woods, green becoming a smell and a feeling rather than a color. I remember hearing once that the oldest preserved smell on record came from a funerary boat found in Cheops tomb. It was forty-six hundred years old. Its scent was as fresh as the days before its wood was cut down.

The green rustles and hisses; it rattles. I read once that physicists have put wooden instruments under electron microscopes and watched them after they were played. They vibrate for thirty-six hours after they have been put down. Wood still lives when it is dead. I feel that here. There are singing generations.

I think of this life in the trees and I am reminded of the wildman, as I so often am when I think of you growing in the shade. In *Wild Men in the Middle Ages* (Harvard, 1952), Richard Bernheimer tells us stories from Switzerland, where the wildman is still celebrated in growing-season dances; there he is called "Fangge," "Fanke," or "Faengge." The wild dweller of the forest is a formidable creature, the stories say; when aroused to anger, he will attack trespassers with his enormous wooden club to protect the forest. In fact, he is bound to such a degree to his woodlands that there are stories of the wildman begging lumbermen not to cut down a tree, as it contained his life substance. They didn't listen; they cut the tree down. The wildman was never seen again by the people there.

But I see him here. There is an emanation of new leaves and honeyed oaks; the attainted ashes of last season and the ghosts of wild ones are audible to me. We stop in the frothed light of the forest, standing within the dolmens of ringed flesh, reaching for the sun and soil.

I watch you pick up a leaf
And quietly study its color,

Expecting Teryk

You had never seen a red leaf before,
You were born in the summer when
The leaf you hold was still high on the tree.

You sat, so tiny,
With your hair shining in the sun
I knew your hand would turn to leather
Changed and wrinkled like the leaf you still hold,

But today you are so young and soft
Against the spent leaves
And I watched you read a young poem
In the cracks and tracing,
And you smiled, finding the secret of birth in its lines.

In an old Norse story, the god Odin breathed on a sapling and made the first man. His name was ask. Since then we have questioned everything, sometimes forgetting to answer the trees that made us. I stand still and listen for the truth.

A thousand years ago, the words for tree and truth were the same. As I stand here I reflect on the truth: that trees were never meant to be alone. I look up into their branches and remember all of the times I have seen single trees in the islands in the streets, standing invisible amid a speed they could never comprehend, like a garnish on a plate—never meant to be taken in, left as decoration at the side. I know I would be alone without them, and I think about how alone they must be without each other.

I have a secret fantasy. When I am old, I would like to climb up into a tree and never come down, just sit there, nearer to the sky, where I could write, receiving wisdom from them, like Odin learning language as he hung in the branches, reading not letters but the space around them as if they were only small cuts in the real story, the crossed and crooked bones of trees.

Maybe I would live an unnaturally long life in the midst of the forest, becoming like the trees. A yew is in its prime when it is five hundred years old, and there are trees on mountaintops that are four thousand years old. In England, trees are considered immortal when, so old that they are rotted out in the middle, they still stand. As an old woman, my legs and veins growing into an immortal tree, I would see stories etched in the leaves around me, and I would press them all. I would put them carefully in an envelope and send them out, my manuscripts. My dendroscripts. My skin would get thinner so I could leak into the world; a blessing my body would give me when I was prepared to pass.

When I was gone I would hang peacefully on some still-living branch, the rest of my body eventually taken whole into the tree. I imagine it crying for me, crying sap tears like the sap that leaks from where we cut.

I stand without moving. I am in company. I think of Odin, barely alive on the tree that will stand until the end of the world, and the gift of the trees to his mind. I think about Christ and the gift that the trees gave to his body, perhaps to his soul, holding him up to heaven. They are always with us.

The dogs and I move down to the ocean, through the sheltering trees and into the hot sun. I can taste it from here—the purling shallows, happy tears moving like serpents through the cool, reaching for my current. Lapping waves of vapor trace their way to the air as it calls them home, and sliding silver shadows break and *ssshhhh, ssshhhh.* They tell us to be quiet. I heed them as the dogs bark, the joyful pounding of their own hearts drowning out the older beat on shoals.

Standing at the end of the trail I see a deep ditch dug next to the beach. Fresh flowers and grass have been dug up and tossed to the side to make way for the dark deep, forming a fresh wound in the earth and a waiting mound of soil. I look at the drying flowers, naked at the roots.

I take the time to lay your book near the hole in the ground and gently pick up the wild flowers at the top of the freshly dug earth, determined to replant them a few feet away. I scoop out a shallow hole of my own and push in the roots of the wilted flowers, covering them as best I can. When I stand back to appraise them, my heart sinks as the last stalk left upright bends and droops, finally surrendering to the ground and kissing it with its soft petals. I sigh.

These are the times I hate everyone. At these times I feel the gashes and cuts and know that they aren't crimes when they are done this way. It is one of the only times I feel disabled. I think disability is about suffering, and usually I turn to the joy of being different, not the pain. But in moments like this I feel crazy, like I could shriek until I foam, could run into walls over and over, no matter who was watching. Why would I care? The people watching me would be the ones who don't even see that the ground bleeds when you claw at it. This feeling usually lasts an eternity of thirty seconds or so, and then I start to fall blindly into the inner shrieking and foaming, running over and over again into the walls in my mind. I count the times I hit and bounce off, the counting necessary. I click my teeth together in rhythm, quietly, so no one will hear. People don't understand that I must do this to bite the feeling off in pieces that won't choke me, that these rituals serve to calm, to center, to soothe me. I do it so that I can come back to the people I love, the people whose love forces me, like birth, to come out and face the world.

I bend and plant myself on the bank near the stony beach, the new, soft reeds beneath me, satisfied that the ground and its growth are holding me in just the right position. My knees are drawn up slightly and my arms are hugged in tight. Warmth is all around me, and I focus on the feel of the lapping waves that stand up to come to shore and dissolve into rock, the sea pouring rhythmically out of itself and always, always, following its outward motion.

I close my eyes, seeing the blood, so like the water of the ocean, between my body and the sun. I know there is a thin layer of salt tears between the red and my eye. I cover my eyes with the backs of my hands and press. Blue lights, like phantoms, swim in patterns, emerging from the darkness. I think of the deep ocean, black and empty like space, a floor as gray and lifeless as the moon. I see slow-moving fish, not ugly in the perpetual night as it hides their huge jaws never shut; their blind eyes carry glowing torches of indigo, the beacons of monsters. Almost motionless on the lunar surface, they know only hunger. They are out there now.

> Early in the banting vessel of my starving,
> I sailed hungry toward the stark,
> My soul a sloop upon an unfed straight,
> A man of war, an ascetic strayed,
> A monk on a slave ship set to straggle,
> As a Lenten drifter turning starboard,
> My fasting became a scowling scow and strained,
> And I was meager, my spareness strange,

My craft and famishment startled
Fore and aft my abstinence stared,
The ketch was spare in its winding trail,
The galley, denied, stared,
At the floating gallery of my drawn wraiths,
Adrift, austere.

I let my deeper thoughts ebb with their own low tide and sit up, blinking under brilliance. The dogs run together, nose to nose, barking with shallow breaths, trying to win, trying to win nothing.

I stand and call them to go. They race to me, their own high tide. As I turn to find the trail I glance at the flowers near the ditch. They are wilted. My heart doesn't sink at the sight; I find the quick waves of time in the inevitability of my prediction, and instead of tears I shed kisses in my mind, letting them go.

I pick one of the bending flowers and look at its color, its veins, so unique and individual. There will never be another exactly like it.

You, my son, now bobbing in the brine of a smaller mother, can flex your arms and clasp your hands. You have developed individual fingerprints unique to you. There will never be another exactly like you. I imagine you curled up, your eyes closed, red between your eyes and the light. You could reach for this flower and hold it, if only I could reach you.

I take your book from my side and open it on the ground, letting it tenderly receive a single flower as I press it closed.

The Dream

I had a dream the other night, the kind of dream that took my soul and left it sleeping in my nostrils in the morning.

I dreamed I was awake as I glided through the darkness of the sun and sussurated through the blinding moonlight, haunting familiar places and places that were not places but still more waking dreams, unfamiliar.

I had no control over my flight as images and scents, distant singing and madness crept into my every open place. It was as if I were a part of someone else's night, and though I begged them to wake, I knew they were asleep and would always be so. And as days, perhaps a thousand years, passed, I found within myself a growing certainty that I was the one who would not open her eyes.

In frosted fields I stood mute as my dream howled at the moon. In warm and soupy seas inside my blood I waited quietly to emerge, gasping, from the ancient salt of my own shore. Hidden within an expanse of dry and whispering grass I called out, as if I was summoning my roaming spirit back before the last meal of the day, the last supper of my knowing.

Foggy shapes passed by me, and, not very often, spoke. They were like the unfocused words of the book I write for you and appeared for an instant to make simple and perfect sense before becoming incomprehensible once more, to stay hidden, confused. Your book was there. I looked down on my pale hands and sometimes could see only the book and not the hands that held it—though I felt them, moving from shattering stiffness to nebulous nowhere. At times it seemed that my hands—or my idea of them—had lived their shape only to become the invisible cradle that held this work, these pages. They blew open now and made a sound like the grass all around.

Someone was speaking.

"There are many different kinds of death to speak about, and we think the one we talk about is permanent, unaware that our words stay and disbelief is a death that bleeds." The voice trailed off even as it grew louder.

I thought of all of the bodily deaths that I had lived through: the multiple punctures of flickering fluorescent lights that stopped my heart from beating behind my eyes, the bludgeoning of clanging school bells that bruised my brain until my consciousness was gone, and the smell of fresh meat, the sweet, dead smell of bleating and silent animals, floating to the bottom of my fortressed mind.

I had tried so desperately when I was younger—a million years ago, when I cared—to tell the people around me what my world was like, how it hurt me, how it delighted me, how it was real though no one else seemed to see it, to know of it. I thought of the times I had died trying to explain myself to people and how I woke up in the telling only to die again when they didn't understand me, didn't believe me. I heard whispering.

I turned my thoughts around, searching for the source of the words in the crimson blowing. From a pool of rose-colored life at my feet I saw a faint trace of a face, then a body of sorts.

"I am visiting you," it said as it took shape. *"I am visiting you . . . "* The misted form rose slowly to stand, its eyes at first parting only a little, then coming open as its face drew close to my own as I sat very still.

The apparition swayed and closed its eyes, a tear of maroon escaping from the corner of one. Its face was blank and smooth, but I felt the figure before me concentrating, touching lightly through memories that perhaps seemed less and less relevant in the timeless tide of salted fire spilling into its recall. It was my own ghost.

"I am greeting you."

I closed my eyes and let the greeting wash over me. I knew that it was a gift; it was a present of memory, of living context, of a body clasping rather than a hand shaking. I tried to greet the apparition in turn, willing my own soul out into the void, feeling defenseless. Then I felt myself expand into something greater—into organisms, tissues of community, a single-minded mass, stumbling forward with sharpened sticks, like a single blind person tapping a deadly spear to this side and that.

Still, I was apart.

"You have always needed distance. You made it just as surely as it made you in the beginning. But oddity isn't in the distance, it's in the kind of distance, the flavor of it that makes you normal or not. The flavor of distance is how a community organizes itself. The codes of distance constitute the law—for the living and the dead."

The floating form behind me hid its face and turned slowly in ascending spirals, then swirled close to the ground, resting.

"How did I die?" I asked quietly. I thought of all the dead before me. The dead of scores of thousands of years ago, sleeping brown people curled up on beds of red ochre, picked flowers all around their long hair, tears from heaven before the ground covered them like a womb, facing west.

The swimming holes near the heart of the apparition opened, and more crimson honey spilled from them, painting the fresh and howling wind a painful shade of red.

Expecting Teryk

I listened as the laughter and crying in the air, in my heart, quieted into bare whispers of story.

"*I was bleeding,*" the wraith cried into the red dark. "*I was alone.*"

After a pause of days, my ghost sighed to me.

"*As I slid under the surface of the rusted dust I heard someone say they were sorry, but no nail driven into the floor could fix me to their remorse, because I could not see it as my own.*"

The wraith seemed to pull into itself, leaving me swimming in a loosened grip, knowing that no harm would come to me. I was resting in peace, in a ghostly state; I knew I would wake up. I knew I was not alone anymore. I dreamed, and the apparition, its voice like my own letting go, went on.

"*The living are always asking for forgiveness, to be excused, always asking for passage; they don't see the bleeding, the bleeding, for which they never seek absolution from one another. In the end it doesn't matter. We all know we were never alone.*"

I felt myself enveloped in a dark and hidden balm. Somewhere in my thoughts I visited the idea that the ghost had not caused my pain, but that what I had felt had been its own pain, already present, leaking out of it on its way home. I let this deeper peace cradle me gently as I listened.

I entertained the idea that ghosts would have no need of community organization as living people think of it since we are all really one thing. Nature or God, our thoughts or the beating heart of time—that is what gives us our order. Our territory is everywhere and nowhere. We have no territory that is not already ours, that will be only ours when they die.

I reflected on my feeling of belonging and the feeling of rightness that held its hand. I had always been alone; rather, I had always thought myself alone among the living. I had a growing realization that I had never been alone, neither was I ill or damaged—I had always been in the company of the disembodied, of the wheeling of the stars.

"Those who were born ghosts welcome every living and dying thing and kiss all that is in between. We divine the future and the past; we shake and throw our own bones and read the signs. We read the tea leaves left by the sea on the shore and run our delicate hands over where the smoke spills and forms." We were kin.

The figure came close to my face and fixed its gray eyes on my own. It hovered there for a moment, looking through me at the whistling world beyond.

"When you suck in your last breath, reversing your first loud exhale, when your naked body shakes, slick with sweat in place of that first wetness, when you have been delivered through that tight, black hole that marks the end of floating at the end of a cord and marks the beginning of your freedom, we will be there . . . we are here. . . . We celebrate, we paint you red and lift you up for all to see; unlike the living, we do not kill things to feast on to celebrate the birth of death, we feast on the cries of the new born, we light tiny places of fire on the layered cake of the grave. We sing the ancient songs that give you your name."

When my eyes cleared of tears, I saw that the apparition was gone. Only your book was clear in my hands. I opened it slowly as its pages blew. The words written on the pages were blurry and secret, as they are in dreams.

. . . sshttofhhwpqmcfny djiuweuhqd, duhjdidqamxfko, ndjmkhfydg, dejifjijdcm, cnjvniahur, djhfuwejt kj wiorjwirejfcw, dueu, ewiejfiw rgjec- nawe rfiqjf, ksjderugr, qrewu hfnvojeigvh, dfuirnfqrjgg, hworiqomdqow . . . Then, suddenly, all the words came into focus for a moment, becoming your name, your story. You would be there at my end.

Expecting Teryk

Sometimes, after I have dreams about you, or even think about you, I feel an interesting anxiety creep into my chest. I can feel it crawling like something with a long, green tail, up and out of my brain stem. As I have always done, I give over to the ritual forcing its way out of deep places where I have no control. It is where animal ritual comes from. Before the pregnancy it was called "obsessive / compulsive behavior." Now it is called "nesting." Either way, it comes from the oldest electrical messages sent up the oldest of wires, from fish to reptiles to birds to mammals to me. Heeding its call, I rearrange the furniture, put the dishes away twice, ready your bed. I count the diapers. I pace. I am in good company among the birds and beasts.

The parts of our brains we share with other animals are the most ancient parts of the human brain: the upper spinal cord—the medulla and pons. The pons lies above the medulla and is made of a bridge of fibers that connect the two halves of the cerebellum, joining the midbrain with the medulla. The structures are what might be considered the "translator" of our breathing, of our beating hearts. Surrounding the midbrain we find the olfactory bulb, the corpus striatum, and the globus pallidus. This is the portion we share with all other mammals as well as reptiles. It evolved several hundred million years ago. This complex acts as the flashpoint of aggressive behavior, territoriality, the establishment of social hierarchies . . . and ritual. At times I can almost feel it pulsing, buried under layers of control, like twisting teeth, telling me to do, to do, to do.

Surrounding the deep structures of the brain is the limbic system. The limbic system probably developed more than 150 million years ago and is made up of several small bodies. The limbic system in its totality is believed to be the translating seat of emotion and the organizer of social interaction in its most primitive forms. Experiments in which areas of the limbic system have been electrically stimulated have produced fear, rage, and sexual urges. This part of my own brain, they say, may be underdeveloped, or perhaps it is overdeveloped. The truth of this depends greatly on whether you believe what experts say about people like me or what I tell you about myself. For me it is enough to know that I cry when researchers say that autistic people lack empathy and then say in the next paragraph that they need to do more experiments on animals to find out why.

Surrounding the limbic system are the cerebral hemispheres, covered by the neocortex. The cerebral hemispheres account for about 80 percent of the human brain. The covering of the cerebral hemispheres, the neocortex, is thought to be the area associated with human intelligence and higher brain functions. Its folds and convolutions are quite similar to those of other higher primates such as the anthropoid apes, but even more complex. It is thought that the neocortex translates information into what we experience as waking consciousness and our linear perception of the world. But though I am very smart indeed it is not the waking but the dreaming that I see when my eyes are open. A consciousness like snakes that never saw the dawn of man, like that of chattering, running things with new fur after the meteor.

We dream together.

You are gaining weight; all your vital systems are in place; the only reason you couldn't survive outside the womb is an inability to breathe. I think about this as I sit in your great-gramma Margaret's project apartment in a haze of cigarette smoke, a chain of fire in my father's mother's mouth. Each time she takes a draw on the perfect white stick in her mouth, it flashes bright orange and I imagine the beats of her heart, after all these years of smoke, beating at the same pace, slow, small, glowing and then almost going out.

She has the shades drawn. It's too bright outside, she says. The shades are the cheap plastic kind, and no air gets into the still, hot, misty womb of her apartment, even though four fans are blowing. Their worth is in making interesting swirls in the smoke, and I get lost looking at them. We are drinking ice tea. Back when she could breathe she made it from scratch, with lots of sugar, but now I make regular runs to the tiny corner store where they have cases only of Coke and Lipton's with lemon. They keep the cases cold there.

Until a few years ago, my Gramma Margaret worked at Dairy Queen. She is proud that she worked there into her sixties; it seemed so much better than the factory work she had done. When I was a kid, we would get treats at what she called, in her thick midwestern accent, "Ma Dae-ree Quane." In the summer, piling into the car in the evening when my father got off from work, we drove into town to the place where the Dairy Queen always stood—my dad always ordering a Coke Freeze, my mother always getting a Dilly Bar, my sister a Mr. Misty Kiss, and myself always a butterscotch malt.

In the wintertime the Dairy Queen stopped serving cold snacks and sold Christmas trees in the parking lot, and we never got one anywhere else. It was years before I knew you could buy a Christmas tree anywhere but Dairy Queen. To me it seemed natural, because they sold Wonderful Things. So when I was little my Gramma Margaret's world always seemed magical, like she lived on Big Rock Candy Mountain where it was always a holiday, or like her shadowbox, which always contained carnival glass angels and fat ceramic Santas year 'round.

When she would watch me when I was little it was like a holiday, too, because we always ate the same thing: creamed corn, fried baloney, macaroni and cheese, and Bunny bread. It was important, she said, to have a nutritious meal. Her grandbabies were going to be healthy, she said. I remember her telling me this as her ubiquitous cigarette dangled and danced on her pale lips, her eyes squinting against the acrid fumes.

I remember when my aunt Gladys died in her seventies, my Gramma Margaret's sister, her friend. Gramma cried on my shoulder for a while and then didn't cry anymore. We went to the funeral home later that day for the viewing. My gramma tried to hide behind me as we sat, several rows back from the casket. She never liked people, and talking to them when her sister was dead in the room seemed ridiculous to her. I told her not to hide behind me because I didn't like people either, and she laughed.

People found us whether we liked it or not, people I had one memory of, no memory of. They were all smiling and patting us, and I started making a game of which sentence each approaching person would use. "She looks so natural." "She's in a better place now." "She's bound for glory."

When it was our turn to go up, we both went together and looked down on Gladys.

"She looks dead," I said.

"Yep," my Gramma Margaret said. We laughed again. Her laugh didn't last, and she held her lips together tight.

Gramma's other sisters showed up. They hugged us and each went to peer at Gladys. I had known them long enough to know that they were whispering, *"She looks dead."* When they came back they didn't stop at their seats. It was an unspoken certainty that they all needed a cigarette, and my Gramma Margaret fell in behind them, and I behind her, though I didn't smoke. Perhaps I needed to be with people who did.

In the parking lot of the funeral home everyone but me lit up, looked away.

"The funeral business is bullshit," one of her sisters announced, blowing out a stream of smoke as forcefully as she had laid out her conviction.

"Lordy, Lordy." Another sister shook her head.

"Don't let 'em do me that way. Just kick me off a truck in a cornfield."

"Helluvalot cheaper. I don't want them bastards gettin' *my* money."

"That sure as shit ain't Gladys in there."

"No. It sure as hell ain't."

Draws from cigarettes melted into drawls in the summer heat. Then it was quiet. I stood downwind of the memories blowing by my head. We all thought of Gladys.

One sister started. "You remember that time Gladys went into town, when we were kids?" And story followed laughter, and laughter followed story in the hot parking lot out in the sunshine. Just past the dark doorway of the funeral parlor we could here somber music falling on deaf ears when everyone would silently agree to stop and take another pull from their cigarettes. Smoke on the wind, leaving the dark.

The next day I took my gramma to the graveside service. They had a preacher. He wasn't a minister or a pastor—I knew the difference—and I wondered where they had found this preacher. I imagined my uncle Francis opening the man's office door, straining to see him through the fire and brimstone that pitched from a wide-open ceiling.

The lid of the casket was open. I put my arm around my gramma. The preacher started.

"The only way we can get to heaven is through BAPTISM. Only by being BORN AGAIN will ye find a way to life EVERLASTIN'," he started, the way only a southern preacher can, spinning damnation out of the most benign of words, wringing them until they cried to heaven for mercy. He leaned back, grimacing, to fix us all with a squint. It looked as though he was shutting his eyes against the stinging curl of smoke from hell.

"Only he who believeth in ME, shall enter the gates of heaven and sit at my father's side," he said dangerously. I wondered about the way he emphasized the word, whether he was quoting Our Savior, or if he really meant that we had to believe in him, the preacher, personally. I suspected the latter.

As the preacher officiously cracked open the Bible to read the passages that demonstrated that the man from Galilee was going to back him up on this one, I looked behind him at Gladys. Gladys had not been what you would call a religious woman. Only, I thought, several pints of formaldehyde would keep her from sitting up and jerking a knot in this preacher's tail. My Gramma Margaret and I looked at each other, but looked away again quickly. We both knew people weren't supposed to laugh at funerals.

After the service Gramma went to sit in the car. I walked up to the casket and put my hand on Gladys's hand, resting neatly on her stomach. It was like touching a mason jar that was empty, between beets and pickles. "You're not here anymore," I said. I just stood there for a minute, being quiet, because she was gone. "I always liked you," I said. "I just wanted you to know."

On my way to the car I met the preacher, putting his Bible away in its velvet case.

"If the only way to our Lord is through baptism, does that mean babies and Buddhists are going to burn in eternal fire?" I asked. I felt sincere. I wanted to know what he thought, so I said it softly.

"Well," he said, clearing his throat and smiling a country smile, "people are only damned if they are given the choice to see the Truth and refuse God out of meanness of spirit."

"So, in other words," I said, looking out at the rolling hills of the cemetery because I couldn't bear to look at him directly, "there are exceptions. Good people who haven't come to the Lord through baptism can still get into heaven?"

He said yes. But he was uncomfortable and wanted to leave.

"I think you should be careful about what you say then," I said more softly still, looking at anything but him.

I knew that if I told him I was gay he would probably not even speak to me. That without even knowing me he would be sure I was going to go to hell, and instead of this kind of eternal damnation evoking sorrow or loss from him, he would be happy to send me down with a can of lighter fluid. Usually that kind of thing didn't bother me, or if it did I didn't allow myself to think about it. There were too many people who wanted me to go to hell. People I would never even meet or know unless I saved their lives by accident, or maybe they saved mine—that kind of intimacy that throws everything into clear relief—but then they would go back to being strangers. Except that I don't know any strangers. I used to say, when I was younger, that if everyone didn't get to go to heaven then I didn't want to go either. I couldn't stand to think of anyone hurting for eternity.

The truth is that people don't hate other people unless they feel like they have been hurt by them. I try to avoid hating people that hurt me, but I know that the people who want me to go to hell must feel that I have hurt them in some way. I was surprised by a scary feeling that I could be lying in Gladys's place without ever having known how I hurt these people. It made me sad.

I had a sudden, overwhelming feeling of love for the preacher. I don't know why. I turned to look him right in the eye. I saw just a man scared of death, scared of life. I put my arms around him and hugged him tight.

"Thanks for everything," I said, and I meant it. I walked away to find the other people I loved.

I found my gramma and her sisters outside the car, smoking. Practice, the preacher would have thought.

"Gladys didn't have nothin' to do with that fun'ral service," my Gramma Margaret declared.

"Lordy, Lordy," a sister said, shaking her head.

"I kept expecting her to sit up and say sit down!" This admission didn't come from me, but from a sister. We all laughed.

"That would have been a good'n!"

"If'n anybody'd a-done it, it woulda been Gladys, I'll tell you what."

We all looked down. Yeah. That was true.

After the funeral we went to my Aunt Gladys's house to eat. It was all there, the food smelling like summer and Thanksgiving and Christmas, angels and Santas all year 'round. Set out on folding tables in the garage were chicken and dumplings, string beans with bacon grease, fancy taters (my aunt Aleyne, who always made these, pronounced both words with a long *a*), pecan pie, and red velvet cake (which took one bottle of red food color per recipe).

My gramma filled a plate and came to sit beside me on the folding chairs outside. We looked out on Gladys's and Francis's farm, over fields of green where I used to catch lightning bugs and the barn where my father used to play, the yard where my grandmother had been a young woman. Her story was all around us, in the land, in the ground, on my plate, in the day.

"I always knew you were quiet because you were thinkin' important things," my gramma said, looking at her dumplings.

"I tried," I said.

"I told people to leave you alone to get on with thinkin'."

"Thanks, Gramma."

"When I die," she said, "I don't want nobody touchin' me. I want a veil over me for the viewin'. I want to be wearin' my pink satin dress, and I don't want no preacher lyin' while I'm a-layin' there."

"Anything else?" I had taken out a piece of paper and started writing down her requests.

"I want you to play Elvis singin' 'Peace in the Valley.'"

"Ok."

She watched me put my paper and pen away. We sat and finished our food.

"Maybe you'll write about your old Gramma Margaret someday," she laughed before looking back out over the fields. "But no. Not really. I'm not that intrestin'. You need to write about big, important things."

"Yes, I do," I said, and I hugged her to my shoulder. "I do."

Gramma Margaret left us. She is lying in Oaklawn Cemetery. She had her way.

I hope I will join her in heaven.

You are now about a foot long, my son, and weigh about a pound and a half. Your eyelashes have grown, and so have your fingernails. Your lungs are developing alveoli, and I think about your future breaths, smelling what I smell in the fall air. If I breathe slowly, I can smell and taste and see a hundred different things in the air—the ghosts of red leaves forgetting green, the caramel waiting of apples and pumpkins, the bedtime stories of growing things. School has started, and I am teaching.

It is my secret pride. I am an anthropologist. I never speak about the feeling to anyone, but to me it is a holy vocation. It is my job to remember —to remember the living and the dead, an endless web of breathing, thinking people stretching back to the beginning of time.

When I was a student I ran through the fields, making fire, wearing skins that weren't my own, flaking stones into tools. People thought I was crazy, flaking away before their eyes like so many shards. My "obsessive traits coming out," they would say. Part of my "condition."

They lock people away for that kind of thing; people who can remember the past, or remember the future, or talk to people on the other side of the world, people who don't look like them, people with hair instead of clothes, with long snouts and no human words, but full of human tears.

I think about the university. I have always liked the parts of school that lock up my body, his mind, keep them from their own harm when I get too wild. In kindergarten I thrilled to the square rooms painted in off colors and the narrow halls saluting at right angles, the strictly scheduled time, having lunch at exactly noon in the light green trays with wells that kept the predictable food of Tuesdays and Wednesdays from touching. And though I hated the noise, the brightness, the rigidity of ideas and minds and desks always rigidly facing forward, I have come back at every point in my life. I have voluntarily committed myself.

Outside the walls of school I would have fallen off the edge of my mind and run naked to dark places, like the ancient voices do as they stalk slippery through my brain. So I go there, even when I don't have to be there, when no one else wants me there. No one notices me today as I sit on a bench, looking at the crowded square. I decide to go and greet the buildings, whose faces never change. Perhaps this is a wild place after all.

Halloween is coming. I can feel it. I walk slowly, savoring the feeling of my own echoes in the rock-face hallways, past classroom caves and forests of chairs. I feel as if every brick, every cornice, every tile has recorded an indelible record of the learning that has happened through the years. They do it silently, unobtrusively, and they quietly offer it back when single, naked footsteps pass by. One has to listen carefully, though, because these shadows of nature speak in a different language.

I let my fingers run over the rough bricks as I walk, pausing to caress a waterfall banister. This looks odd to the passing students, so I walk on, consciously keeping my steps steady. In this way I talk to the buildings.

I dread the first day, meeting a group of students I am going to teach about primate behavior. Everyone's eyes stick to me as I levitate through the door and walk to the back of the room, where I continue to stand blankly. I avoid the glances, the stares, the lingering appraisals, thinking it is a sad commentary that I am suddenly the most interesting thing in the room.

I feel an increasing sense of euphoria as each pair of eyes drops from their search of me in turn and releases me from the scratching, the bruising, the tearing that always occurs when another person eats the light coming from my body. I feel a balm of relief cover the temporary wounds of piercing eyes, the stigmata of my projected image.

Sometimes, in these situations, I have fallen off the edge of myself. When this happens I stride quickly out of the room, followed by a sudden, low buzz of swarming conjecture that makes everything worse. I go and sit in my favorite stall in the bathroom with my hands over my eyes. I think hard about the importance of teaching people to understand old and wild things. I go back.

Now, remembering their importance, I navigate through a class, and it is like the final push through a birth canal or some ancient cave: my exposed edges are smoother, leaving no purchase for the grasping walls pushing in on me. I am surrounded by the lubrication of routine and slide through to the daylight at the end. All my spirit has to do is keep its eyes shut as it clamps itself into a small ball and waits for time.

Today I write on the board with chalk, though the gritty feeling makes my teeth hurt. It helps to think of the chalk skeletons of a million ancient organisms who had, perhaps, a very different sort of fear as they swam blind and deaf in thick, forgotten pools; they could bear only blind witness. They continue to bear blind witness now as the students look at their white bodies trailing lifelike on the black instead of mine. I am talking about evolution. I never know how to figure out what the students know and what they don't know; I can't imagine what they think as I talk. I wonder if I should start at the beginning, in a muddy brine that sounds like rot, a spasm half-living in the quicksand. Should I start with the steaming froth like a sticky and swimming shiver, shaking in its own fog, in the musk of a million wet, white bellies and crawling legs? I hear a tumulus of thunder, a draughting rain.

There is the murmur and hum of a cloud of chirrups caught in my throat. In the silence I hear a car drive by the building and think of black bogs and long-dead frogs, making crude oil, their spirits refined into gasoline, to burn. I imagine the roar of engines as the wail of a billion tiny living things from a dim past, telling their story with the only voice that's left to them. I think of the phantasmagoria, the machines that projected ghostly images to sellout crowds in the nineteenth century, yesterday.

I am lost in a forest of the tertiary, when horsetail ferns were as big as trees and there were no birdcalls, only the yawp of warm things and the silent glide of cold sharks, the slither of giant salamanders ten feet long and a thousand pounds.

A student asks a question, and I am here. I have been gone only seconds. That is how time works in the past. Where we come from can change us so quickly, everywhere and everywhen is in us, present. Perhaps that is why ancient people believe the souls of the dead lived on in their tombstones, the teeth of God.

I decide to start with our recent past. When I speak out loud, my words seem too black and white, as if there is something missing in the middle.

"Five million years ago," I say, "we begin to see all the building blocks of our culture, building blocks we share with apes who have evolved and who themselves still lean on the older ways, nurturing an old culture still new to them."

I put a list of cultural behaviors on the overhead projector. Each word is a fossil belonging to every person living, and in some form, each of these we share with living apes and the ancestors we share.

age grading	inheritance rules
athletics	joking
bodily adornment	kin groups
calendars	kin terminology
cleanliness training	language
community organization	law
cooking	luck superstitions
cooperative labor	magic
cosmology	marriage
courtship	mealtimes
dancing	medicine
decorative art	modesty
divination	mourning
division of labor	music
dream interpretation	mythology
education	numerals
eschatology	obstetrics
ethics	penal sanctions
ethnobotany	personal names
etiquette	population policy
faith healing	postnatal care
family	pregnancy usages
feasting	property rights
fire making	tool making
folklore	trade
housing	visiting
hygiene	weaning
incest taboos	weather control

"The list we see here includes every component known to make up culture. Each and every one of these elements is present in every culture we know of." I switch on a projector and click through slides, ticking them off with my mental stopwatch. *Stop. Watch.* I think. I think about the archaic building blocks of family; it is sprinkled like a salted fire through the forms of what I say.

"Some of these component behaviors are readily identifiable. I am confident that such things such as courtship . . ." *Click. An Egyptian statue depicting lovers.* ". . . dancing, family . . ." *Click. A picture of a Peruvian weaving bearing colorful figures in captured motion. A Malaysian man holds his infant daughter close.* ". . . feasting, fire making . . ." *Click. An Australian Aboriginal family sleeps next to a tiny center of flames.* ". . . games, joking, kin groups and kin terminology . . ." *A Mexican family celebrating at a fiesta.* ". . . and law, marriage, mealtimes, music . . ." *A Ukrainian man plays an instrument as his wife looks on, making bread.* Every few words I pause to clear my throat. I know it is distracting, but I can't help it. I hope the slides I am clicking through hold the students' attention.

I point out other concepts that I know from experience that the students, who are members of the family of humanity, will identify. ". . . cooperative labor . . ." *Click. Basque men help to repair a broken wagon.* ". . . folklore . . ." *Click. An image of the wildman from a French church.* I click at a steady pace, breaking time into manageable bits for both my own sake and theirs. ". . . hospitality . . ." *Click. An Inuit man offers whale blubber to a friend.* ". . . hygiene, incest taboos, inheritance rules . . ." *Click. A picture of Trobriand Islander women giving away wealth in the form of skirts and banana leaves.* "Personal names, postnatal care, pregnancy usages, property rights, puberty customs . . ."—I clear my throat. I could go down the list in my alphabetically organized dreams I know it so well. ". . . sexual rules, community organization . . . " *Click. A photograph of a Chinese Emperor's tomb.* ". . . trade, visiting . . . " *Click. A Sammi woman from Scandinavia offers a dish of food to another woman.* ". . . weaning . . . " I pause as the students scribble notes, their eyes moving from the pictures to their notebooks, as if the act of transferring the words made them real. That was another behavior I suspected should be on the list, but it wasn't. I absently wonder why as I steel myself against the scratching of pencils, like biting insects filling my ears. I focus on the peace of a slide of a Hawaiian grandmother with her grandson. ". . . luck superstitions and mourning . . . " *Click.* The students lean forward. The image is small and far away. They can't make out the details, though this slide interests them more than the others. Silently I wonder how many of the students, darting glances, scribbling quickly, had mourned, and wonder what they mourned most often, most deeply. I wonder which ones had been lucky, which ones had families that were alive and healthy. Where there is plenty there is also loss. The faces turn down and away from me, though I think I see mourning's night in clear and subtle paints over a person here, a person there. I look just as carefully for joy, lost in my task, until one by one each face rises to meet me and the shadows of silent searching give way to equally searching eyes. Yes. They are the family of humanity. Soon I will know what that really means, what that really means.

"Every culture we know of has some kind of family unit. Whether the people are wealthy . . . " *Click. An American mansion.* ". . . or have what the land offers them . . . " *A dwelling of the San of the Kalahari—simple piles of grass over very shallow pits scraped in the ground. Click. A comparative slide showing an Inuit snow hut of the arctic next to a house on poles in the rainforests of Cambodia.* In all of the pictures families look into the eye of the camera, greeting the other families of the rest of the world. I look at the babies in the pictures, naked where it is warm and bundled where it is cold, always wrapped in the heat of those who stand and look out their front doors.

"Most families in the world focus on raising children and invest a great deal of energy in ensuring the health and well-being of their children from the beginning. Obstetrics are, of course, the practices associated with pregnancy, labor, and delivery, usually involving the administration of specific medicines and rituals thought to ensure the health of the mother and baby. There are also various kinds of wisdom passed along through generations regarding nutrition, positions for labor, and other facets of childbearing." *Click. A Scottish woman holds her newborn baby to her chest.*

"Once a child is born, people all over the world have greatly varying ways of taking care of that child in many different kinds of families. Among the Mundurucu of the Amazon, mothers and children live in houses apart from others until the children are thirteen years old, whereupon the male children go to live with the men of the village. In consanguinal families, like those of the Tory Islanders living off the coast of Ireland, people live with their brothers and sisters, even after marrying, which they do later in life. Among the Tory Islanders, children are brought up in their mother's families.

"In avuncular families, like those of the Trobriand Islanders, children are born into a group of relatives who trace their route of descent through their mothers. Property passes to them from their mothers and is watched over by their maternal uncles; leaders pass their rights and responsibilities down to the sons of their sisters." *Click. A picture of a Trobriand Island family in front of a steep and narrow wooden house, painted brightly and reaching tall into the sky.*

"An example of the extended family can be found among the Maya of Guatemala, where sons bring their wives to live in houses that are built

Expecting Teryk

on the edge of a familial plaza along which their father's house is already standing. Women and men tend to their chores in the plaza together as all the children play together. If we look at the Hopi of Arizona, we see that a grandmother is the head of an extended family, joined by her married daughters and their husbands and all of her grandchildren." *Click. A Hopi family sits on the roof and stairs of an adobe structure.*

Another click. A picture of my family when I was a child. "Though it is increasingly rare, some families of non-native Americans are extended families. I grew up with my mother's parents and my mother's uncle, who all lived together." I click forward to a picture of Tara and me standing beside a cradle. I tell them about my new family and about how I miss the old one.

I pause. Questions? No. They have no questions.

I manage a cursory scan of the blank faces. Time is up, and they are anxious to leave the room. Their restlessness is infectious, and I feel the stress tightening my own chest. I glance out the window and see the honey-colored leaves sweetly falling in front of windows, in front of doorways. I think of family, of ancestors, of the people everywhere celebrating the families now dead with the families now living. What the students are thinking I don't know. They melt into one and then divide again like tiny universes created by Vishnu's breath. They go dark.

"You may leave." I hope they are going someplace where people love them, where they have families of the heart.

In a great and coordinated movement, the animated component of the class, the legs and arms and lungs and fingers and the twenty pairs of eyes, rises up in an obliterating wave and rushes through the door. I wait for Halloween. The veil is thin.

The Wild Things Come Home

October 20, 1998

The sun, for many days now, has glittered on the wings of dragonflies and warmed the webs of spiders, as dragonflies and spiders weave endless rings in the water, on the sky, saying goodbye to the year. As I write I wonder if it is really cooler or if my skin, befriending the taming cold of winter, is anxious to meet the true cold of this season. The sun is too bright today, one of its last bright days, and I close my eyes for a while and push on them with my hands like I have done since I was a child and wanted to get away from too much; I enjoy the swirls of blue throbbing and roiling behind my closed eyelids—like the churning at the unfound places beneath water, between continents, before the snow. I open my eyes and watched the last of the swirling apparitions leave the edge of my vision. I could see in them the steady pulse of my heartbeat.

I stand in a stream going out to the ocean. My feet are stiff and pale and slippery, in mute sympathy for other cold and pale slippery things that are coming this way, returning to the cold as I return to the heat. The salmon have come back, like red and slicing stigmata standing out against the skin of the stream, ignoring the plainer colors of a life given up for a holier purpose.

The blood and pumping of their bodies is a silent bleeding, leaking out of them like their unseen tears, new water, new life; a promise fulfilled by a sacrifice kept. In the sun I hum to myself, as I so often do, of things old as if they were new.

Swimming up from darkling streams,
Where only calling swims in dreams,
And shouts so softly to the coming back
That whispers of birthplaces sound like screams,

That is why I was born without ears,
It is with my soul that I hear end near,
In a deafening torrent without any time
The echo, calling, comes down through years,

Water and calling follow me back,
Swimming from darkling, to darker, to black,
Unleash the white slickness that pushes me up
Then back and away to the swimming attack,

Without seeing, or hearing, or tasting, or rest,
Climbing a vision of passing to death,
To the source of the start, to swim for the life,
We swim without blinking in the drink of the blessed,

We raise our lips now to the cold of arrival,
And gulp the wine springing from spawn and survival,
We eat our own flesh as a sacrament living,
Then give up our spirits to dreams of revival.

I look down and at the water swirling around my pink ankles and squat, so that I am almost sitting in the cold eddy and splash of the raging stream that was so low, so secretive only short weeks ago, before the fall rains came. I put my face close so I can smell the water—a swampy smell of remembering water running over the spirit of the dust of the rocks, the dry scent of winter becoming a heady liquor of liquid and breeze.

This scent has backwashed in my dreams in recent nights, and the sound of bubbling, bursting water sweeps away my cares of cold. My senses are drunk with the birth waters flowing both ways, to the womb and from it, from warm to cold and back again.

My slow breath sends ripples along the mirror of the moving surface, making one tiny movement become many more, my breath leaving the keeper of the cave to tend to the future.

An orange leaf, blown from a dozing tree, rushes under the bridge behind me, spinning on the water's rills and dips. It rests against my leg, then is caught again by the wind or current, sailing. Still spinning in circles, it bobs down, away and out of sight, another traveler to the end. I watch the rings that the leaf leaves behind coming into the rings left by my breathing.

I think about the symmetry that the leaf remembers: trees and fish both grow rings—one in the round trunk straining to return to the birthing air, one growing rings in scale and bone, straining to return to the birthing waters, both showing secrets of how old they are on the inside.

I feel the rings that have grown in my own heart, invisible to the naked eye. I think about the rings that my naked eyes have grown, steady around the edge, just out of sight. They are the rings that keep you safe as fall turns to winter and you become a man in my mind, swimming home.

Expecting Teryk

The Wildman Is Bleeding

I, the one of memories,
From ancient earth and ancient seas,
My salt and blood return,

In memories I feel the earth,
The dark enfolds, unfolds the birth,
And ancient fires burn,

In memories I feel the fire
In dreams once buried, I rise higher,
And from the wind I learn,

In memories I feel the wind,
Ancestors sigh and sing again,
The songs the sea discerns,

In memories I feel the sea,
My ancient blood inside of me,
The tides, the phases turn,

I, the one of memories,
From ancient earth and ancient seas,
My salt and blood return.

I just happened upon a beautifully written piece of writing from a website called "Celebrating Autistic Parents" (http://cap.autistics.org/). It was a son talking about his father, who had Asperger's Syndrome. In it, the son called his dad "Mountain Man" and set to remembering how, from the time he could remember, his father would go alone into the mountains. There were times he would take the whole family, ushering them into the forest along with him, under the protection of his arms, his expression protected under his thick beard. His father had to get away from the city, to swim back to his source.

The man's father had had anger problems at one point, but he was a just man and had learned to control his temper, a living example to his children. He became, as his son said, less volatile but not less autistic. He showed his children the value of honesty. Mountain Man's son said that he appreciated that he knew he could rely on what his father said as the truth, a comfort in a world where people often deceive, even when there isn't good reason.

The anonymous author of this reflection said that his father taught him about fairness and equality and bravery—about speaking up when it is the right thing to do. It was clear this son loved his father, as he called him gentle, loving, and compassionate.

I was so happy to find this tribute, as it gives me hope that I will be a good parent to you and that, like the salmon that can taste to clear water, smell their homes and see their homes far away, your own life will guide you to become the good parts of me when you come home to yourself.

I think about your senses now. My son, my tiny wildman, you can see, hear, smell, taste. You are breathing, grasping, turning your head, sucking your thumb, and blinking. You are getting smarter as major changes happen in your nervous system. Your brain is growing so fast that it is folding in on itself, creating the gyri, or wrinkles, so recognizable in the brains of thinking things. The alveoli of your lungs are producing a surfactant, one that is similar to the substance that keeps soap bubbles from collapsing, to keep the air sacs from collapsing. It makes me think of you blowing bubbles with full lungs, drifting on the fall wind turning to winter. The snowflakes will be blowing. The mountains are already white.

November 19, 1998

I look out the window and think about things that come back, things that leave, things that are really gone, and things that one thinks have left forever only to return again. Fish, my grandmother, the year, memories.

I went shopping today for baby supplies. I took a list with me, torn from a book about having babies and what they need. I threw the rest of the book away. I think it's up to me to figure out how to raise a child—after all, everyone is different and some are more different than others. A book like the one I found the list in sure wouldn't have helped my mom.

I hadn't really looked at the list until I got to the store, and as I scanned it while I stood in between two huge aisles of wipes, toys, and Pedialyte, I realized that it wasn't going to help me much either. The list stated with an air of final authority that expecting parents needed ten blankets, a large box of disposable diapers, ten bottles with rubber nipples, twenty washcloths, a bassinet with bumper guards, at least ten baby gowns, baby socks, baby mittens, baby sweaters, several hats, a baby-sized grooming kit, and a booger sucker . . . the list took up an entire page in small print. I suddenly had a suspicion that the book was put out by the plastics industry.

I let the hand holding the list drop to my side. *What do women do in countries where they can't get this stuff?* I wondered out loud. I put the list back in my pocket. *As long as they have food and shelter, they do very well.* I decided that I would have to trust my instincts about this, too.

I walked over to the blankets. Order and symmetry always capture my attention, and I liked the way they were neatly stacked. I ran my hand over their predictable fuzziness, avoiding touching the ones that were yellow —it was a color I had never liked—but when I touched a sea-green blanket I was suddenly in the middle of an old memory. I was a baby. I was lying on

Expecting Teryk

the floor of my gramma's house on a sea-green blanket like the one I was touching; the news was on the television in front of me, and my grampa was sitting near me in a chair. I could smell the laundry soap on the blanket, I could hear the news, I could taste the taste of baby breath in my mouth, like milk made sweeter. Then the memory faded. I put the blanket in my basket.

My memory works that way. I touch an object or see something, hear something, and I am locked into a remembrance that plays out like a four-dimensional movie, like I am swimming in an artifact that has become a mirror all around me, without seam. It is a happysad thing. I am there again, in my favorite places, but then lose them all over again without the muting of time to raise my arm in a goodbye wave behind me.

I reach for a blue bottle on the shelf near the blankets. I had one just like it, I remember, but I haven't touched one since I was four years old. Not caring who is watching, I lift it slowly to my lips. As soon as the smell of the rubber nipple reaches my nostrils I am in the middle of memory again. I am sitting on a gray carpeted floor, building something important with Tinkertoys, the sound of country music playing on the radio in the background, Johnny Cash, I think it is. I can feel the red and blue wooden rods in my hands. They are firm in my fingers. In my mind's eye I glance to my side. My blue bottle is there.

I sigh. I put the blue bottle in the basket, too, though I know Tara will breastfeed. It is too important a memory to leave on the shelf.

When I pass a display of baby food I close my eyes and search my files. My brain can work like a computer. I look at the categories going by like a rolodex. I am looking for "What I Liked to Eat When I Was a Baby." I find it. Chicken. Peas. Sweet potatoes. Bananas.

I reach for a little jar full of pale beige. I reflect that I am glad bananas aren't yellow on the inside. I twist open the tiny glass container and poke in a finger, bringing it to my lips. I am in a high chair at the corner of a chrome dinette, my mother spooning creamy bananas into my now small mouth. I bang on the tray in front of me. My mother smiles. I can't understand what she is saying.

But what my mother is thinking comes back to me, what she was doing, what she has done. And what her mother is saying in my mind, and my father, and his father and his mother also. They have fed me so many things, covered me in blankets warm and sometimes darkening, nursed my needs and fears.

My grandmother herself grew less and less fond of leaving the house until her fondness was for nothing and her world shrunk and she returned to the womb, seeing and hearing nothing. She was pulling away even when she was mothering my mother, pushing my mother away from her belly as she herself returned to it during a gestation of many panicked years; pushing away my mother's brother until he collected a love of guns, of motorcycles, of food. He stayed home, in the home of his birth, after my grandparents were gone, crying bitter tears and rage that things had changed. I share his sorrow because I love him so for his playfulness and embrace on the other side of his pain. My grandmother gave birth to children who would and would not give birth to their own, waiting to grow past the affection they didn't feel, knowing it was there.

Perhaps my mother still waits for it, practicing its coming as she struggles to tell us she loves us, hugs us with arms shedding the loss of something bigger. Instead of kissing the fullness of a warmth pleasing and past, she folds her laundry perfectly, does the dinner dishes in the right order, takes too much time shopping.

To me, my mother's mother was a joy in her isolation: she sat in the same place at the table, said goodbye to leaving and stayed put, giving me gravity like a black hole and mystery that is too distant to affect. My mother was odd and wonderful and her systems imposed order on a chaotic world. She would teach us to pull sweet nectar from honeysuckle and tell us to go play in the traffic. She routinely told my sister and me that she never had liked us, and that would make us laugh. She liked her solitude and made up an imaginary friend for my sister whom my mother would make call my sister into the other room to play by whispering my sister's name through the side of her mouth: *Beanie . . . come play with me . . .*

I think of my father's mother. To me she was the person who made macaroni and cheese for me three times a day if I wanted, the woman whose life fit into a shadowbox, who avoided people as much as I wanted to. To my father she was the woman who didn't know where he roamed in day or in night, his heart beating fast in the cold by the railroad tracks, under the moon, staying away because his mother was also the woman who didn't know when to leave the man who beat her, who beat him. And to me my father is the boy who never grew up and who fought me like a weak kid on the playground, telling me the most marvelous stories when I cried, when I was ready to head into the night alone.

Because he survived he believed that anything was possible. He put a small wiring cap next to my bed one night and told me that if I believed hard enough in the morning I would see it had turned into a kite.

I'll fly away, oh Glory,
I'll fly away,
In the mornin'
When I die, Hallelujah, by and by,
I'll fly away

Perhaps my father, my mother, my mother's mother, my father's mother, all want to return to a heaven only some of them believe in and all of them deserve. I cover myself with the blanket of their trying, drink the milk of their regrets. I eat what they gave me, their faults flavor and their love leaves aftertaste. I throw away the list of what I am told I need for a baby.

Things are moving this season. Things are leaving the sun and following the sun.

I remember hearing about a whole family of autistic people who left everything and fled to the woods deep in the heart of Canada, and sometimes I dream about that. Living next to a den of bears, on a lake with twenty-two thousand miles of shoreline, they call to me, these people who chop their own wood, starting fires even when it is damp, knowing from instinct when a squirrel is dying. It feels like something I have lost rather than something I have never sought.

I think about our ancestors following the bison and the mammoth and the deer as they chased the melting sheet of ice, the great glaciers of the last ice age, northward thousands of years ago. In my mind's eye I see the massive wall of blue and green breathing, its thunderous chest pushing out over the plains of the land, then retreating, only to breathe an icy breath and swallow up the land again. Glaciers pulsing forth like living rivers, slow and throbbing; it would at times move toward us the length of one person in a year and then, by cold magic, would chase us back the length of several hundred people in the same span of time.

Our people came from far away and returned there, too, from the highest mountains in that direction, to the warm lands beyond the hills. We met the sea in the west until we could go no farther. We traveled long distances in the birth of winter and though we were many together, some went here and some went there, calling.

In the summers we lived in the heat of the land, following the yellow of the burning sun, faces painted blue, like the sky. We could see so far—for miles and years, to the back of us and forward. We hunted. Nothing could escape us because we could see the future, our spears flying out of the clouds and into our souls. It was important to be together then, because when something so big as a mammoth dies, it leaves a hole as large, and we had to fill those holes with spirit, with song. We danced and called until we were a part of the stars and no more pieces were missing.

When the autumn came and the days grew shorter with the encroaching night, we flew from the center of the early eve, and at the edge of the deepening blue we would sing among the branches under the harvest moon, like birds who listen to the calling forth of the earth and know where to go without knowing how. The people and the animals in those days made a white blanket of spirit on the land. It is like hovering birds that time flies.

I think of you, my son. You spend 90 to 95 percent of your time sleeping. Babies at this stage have REM sleep—they dream. I wonder if you dream of growing, of being born, of flying south and away. I dream that you and I turn into geese in the shortening days, healing our hunger as our dreams chase them over the whitening land.

I see them flying over as I walk, formations of beating hearts and beating wings suspended above the earth. I smell the wending perfume of soft down when I close my eyes, I breathe in their peppered pine and the bent boughs and sighing skies. My spirit writhes with an ache to soar between where the sun rises on the right and sets on the left, to be a flying wraith, beating buoyant wings like washed white winters iced with gray. I call to them as they peel and bell. They answer only themselves.

Expecting Teryk

I listen closely and believe there is more than the honking we hear with one ear, the other turned away. These birds dream of ancestors, too; of the flying, untethered leather wings of dinosaur birds seeking an end to journey over seas of old and seas of time. The story is long. They tell it now.

My heart seems to know that they sing this story each year, telling of a time before wings with the first note as they lift into the sky, each one of them memorizing and singing a special part, each one flying to the front, taking turns singing its part; chapters of the first fearful flying through the air, the first fine feather, the first fanning flocks of family. They make the story whole and ending with this day when they land at the end of flight.

My heart seems to know that they add to the story each year—chapters of cheating death, of changing charts, of chasing, of children. We are the same. The wild of the woods isn't far away, it is inside me.

Footfalls Soft

Listen, listen,
Hear the sound,
Snow is falling,
Kiss the ground

Quiet, quiet,
Footfalls soft,
Holy sky,
The ghosts aloft

Spirits, spirits,
Fall to earth,
Haunted flakes,
Of white rebirth,

Watching, watching,
All lie still,
Great white blanket
Waits until . . .

Running, running,
In white packs,
The book of earth
Will read our tracks.

Expecting Teryk

There was a windstorm yesterday. It was fierce, like winter's deep breath, and lasted, moaning and tossing, through the night. Tara and I went to the park and gathered branches to make our own Christmas tree since it makes Tara sad to cut down a small living tree, especially now, as we think of your life just starting.

I used rope to tie the branches together and also to tie them to the wall. We made some warm cider with cinnamon and cloves and drank it while we trimmed our Christmas branches. I like unpacking the ornaments and remembering so many seasons past, leading to this one, a season of celebrating a birth. I celebrate them all.

We are sitting quietly on the couch, looking at the twinkling lights and the still ornaments, shining and seeming to have memories of their own. They seem like their own favorite things as they hang there.

I think about my own favorite things, the ornaments of my mind; I walk around the winter-blown boughs of my own comfort, looking at them. I think about my favorite artist, Andrew Wyeth, and the way he can make life out of four shades of green and four shades of brown. He invites me in, gentle to my senses where other colors sting, letting me be there, walking away from me with brush still in hand, a shadow with its back turned, offering peace.

I think about my favorite composer, Vivaldi, who breathes so well through his music that no one remembers that he had asthma and couldn't take in air. I think of luna moths, my favorite flying things, so rare that I have only one memory of seeing one, when I was younger, as green and wide as springtime, its fluttering recalling every leaf that ever rustled, then it was gone behind the purple irises that were also my favorite.

As I sip my hot cider in the candy-colored dark by Tara's side, I think of other favorites, the other ornaments of a life. Ray Bradbury, Suzanne Paola, Zero bars, cream soda, Uranus, amontillado, Nikola Tesla, Paul Feyerabend.

We leave the warm of the flashing pink and green and blue to go outside where the stars, every color, twinkle in infinite strings. We are going to go sledding, and my father has already gotten all of the antique wood and metal sleds out of the chicken coop. Each has a name: Streakin' Ethel, Little Joe, Fightin' Jack Dumpsey (my father found it in a dumpster many years ago, on his way home from work), and Rosebud.

My mother and I stuff our pockets with candles and matchboxes and tramp out into the dark, the air taking our breath away. Silently we move down the long driveway in the blackness, stopping here and there to stick a candle in the snow at the side of the road and then light it. I feel the itch and tickle of snowflakes, tiny reliquaries of light, on my upturned face as we turn upward, our task complete.

The only sound is that of our breathing as we struggle back up the long hill toward the house in the glimmer of starred filigrees around points of light, the house at the end. The Christmas tree is in one window, and its warm lights shine out in the neat squares of the window, making framed and frozen watercolors of home and Christmas on the snow beyond the front.

My father is standing there; his breaths come out in small puffs as he runs the old bar of wax over the runners of the sleds, now turned with their backs against the house. The bar of wax is the same one we use every year, with a deep groove on one side where the runners slide in their familiar track, anxious for speed and curve, waking up.

I look into the sky. An early moon is rising to wax in the waning sky. I think of something I had once read about monks at Canterbury seeing an explosion on the moon sometime around 1100 AD. They were afraid to write down what they had seen, as it was considered heretical to suggest that the heavens changed or hosted events; what was seen through the eyes of living men and revealed by God to them in their waking thoughts on earth was all that was real, all that was ordained. But some brave monk wrote down what he had seen, a message in a bottle to future minds awake and seeing in new ways. With the advent of laser technology, measurements were taken over time that determined the moon's distance form the earth, and it was revealed that there was a slight wobble in the moon's orbit that originated with a tremendous impact around the time of the monks. They were vindicated. This kind of providence always settled a feeling of contentment in me, like being thickly covered in a snow of clean truth—a truth made up of tiny individual thoughts and history, making everything rest under one color.

I look out on the still, white blanket of snow, all the same and all different in the dark. I pick up some snow in my hand. It is cold enough that individual flakes hold their shape, the light lemon and maple taste of only knowing cold, a metallic traid of frozen motion.

> *They came down,*
> *The souls of one snow,*
> *And their whispered prayers*
> *Melted on a forgiving breast*
>
> *A hushed sea*
> *Without wave*

But a still
And frozen froth
Of waiting for an answer,

They fell close together,
Until their was no point,
Just silence,
Just the same.

You have developed fingerprints, small and pale and white, also hidden in the dark. Like you they are distinctive, one of one, one in a million, all looking the same from space, where the earth hangs like a favorite ornament in the heavens.

We are all in the darkness and shimmer now, my mother, my father, my sister, Tara, and within Tara's warmth, you. We start the ritual.

"So which one did we decide was the fastest sled?"

"Little Joe."

"No. Fightin' Jack is the fastest, then Streakin' Ethel. That's why we named them Fightin' Jack and Streaking Ethel."

Part of the ritual is my mother's skepticism.

"No. It's Little Joe."

"Ok, Mom. You get Little Joe then."

"But I don't like going too fast."

"Ok. Take Streakin' Ethel."

"Streakin' Ethel is too fast."

She settles for Rosebud. She throws herself down on the old sled, lying still for a long time. Our breaths still puff in the still air as she takes her time. She tucks in her coat. She wipes her nose. She pulls her gloves tighter. She pushes her hat back on her head. She slides to the front of the sled. She slides to the back. My sister can't stand it anymore.

"What the hell are you doing?"

"Adjusting."

My sister starts to make fun of her.

"Protein pills? Check. Flashlight? Check. Anti-nausea suppositories? Check."

My mother lifts her middle finger in Davina's direction.

"Fuck off? Check."

We all laugh. Dad shoves Mom off the hill. She screams as she launches into the darkness. Another ritual.

We all go down in different combinations, Tara with her big belly standing halfway down, near the middle candle, cheering us on as we whiz past. Davina flies down the hill, lying on Dad, who lies on his stomach on Fightin' Jack; I with mom lying on me, streaming over the hill on Streakin' Ethel; then me with Dad behind me on Little Joe and Davina alone, on Rosebud. We meet at the top of the hill and go down in a chain. The air bites us and whistles in our ears. I have never gone so fast.

The cutting of the curves sends a spray of ice into my face and I laugh out loud, feeling scared of the speed and ready to go faster. Past the shoot and spray I hear my sister laugh in front of me, I hear my mother scream behind me, I hear my father whoop—I can't tell where he is. At the bottom we stand together in the gelid flush of a long time in the welcome chill.

We talk and laugh more as we tramp up the hill again, talking about nothing. Dad reminds me that there is pumpkin pie waiting for us. I feel like a child given more time in the twilight. I smile. I am not ready to go in.

We go down alone, in twos, in threes. I go down with my mother, she is lying on my back as we fire through the night, taking shaking lefts and chopping rights as snow blinds us. My mom is screaming in my ear as she leans too far one way, then too far the other, and I struggle with all my strength to keep the streaking sled upright. I start laughing, then she laughs, too. We start laughing so hard I can't steer, and we roll into a rocketing turn, my mother, the sled, and me, bursting apart in an explosion of powder. Over the bank, over the sled, over Mom I spin, still laughing, until I lie still on my back, looking up at the twinkling stars. I just lie there, panting.

"Are you ok?" My mom looms into view over me, stretching out a hand, snow stuck to her mouth and hat. She's still laughing.

"Yeah. Nothing broken."

We walk up the hill, Fightin' Jack and Streakin' Ethel behind us like faithful dogs.

"I wish my mother had done this kind of thing," my mother says, a little sad, though she's smiling.

"Yeah, Mom, me too," I say. "For your sake and hers also."

"Well, she loved me though." My mom looks at me in the candlelight. I know that she has made this enough, that she made it enough years ago.

"Yeah. She did."

"I made pie," my mother says.

"Because you love me."

"No. Because I love pie."

We start laughing again. I am glad she is beside me.

I rest with Tara, falling in beside her and letting my mother go to the top to ride down with my sister. I put my hand on her stomach.

"Teryk will really enjoy this someday."

"Yes he will."

We have been out a long time. Dad asks me to go down one last time with him. I slog up the hill and lie on his back. He has rewaxed Streakin' Ethel, and the snow is packed tight now. We will fly.

Mom pushes us off, using my feet as luge handles. She runs until she falls and we are already going fast. My dad tells me to hang on tight. I blink and squint as we hurdle dangerously through the air and the freeze. The candles become small streaks and then there are no more. We have flown past them and are banging around blind curves, into the forest. We can't see.

For long moments there is no light at all, and I know Dad is steering the twists by memory only as tight needles of cold and snow pepper my face. I sense that his eyes are shut, and I know he is imagining he is in space, far away, with nothing on his back.

Finally we miss the road and jump the rise at the side, flipping and bouncing, until we stop in the newly scarred white. My father yells that it is a record and jumps up in triumph. I wonder if he is talking about the distance or the time he got to spend in the dark of space, free. We pat each other on the back and turn into the long walk up the road. We are looking at the stars.

"Crazy to think about, isn't it?" he says, out of breath.

"What?" I ask, huffing out the words as my lungs burn.

"Photons. They travel billions of miles through black space and land inside our eyes, inside us."

"Some part of them makes it into us to stay," I reflect, thinking about Christmas lights and candles.

"Yes."

We walk even farther. He speaks again.

"If you took all the space out of all the atoms that make up the earth, the whole planet would fit in a teacup."

"I've heard that." I think about God taking a sip. Ah. Just right.

My mom meets us halfway down. She is picking up the candles. Dad takes my sled in his free hand and pulls both to the house as I go back down the hill. We blow out the candle at the end of the road and pick it up. In the darkness I bump into my mother.

"I love you," I tell her.

"You just covet my sled." She is talking about Little Joe. It is slowest, but the ritual for next year starts here. I laugh.

One candle is left, and I bend to get it as Mom goes on up the hill without me. I lift the candle from its little cave and blow it out. The end still glows red, its light traveling to me over a billion miles. *I am looking into the past,* I think. I blow on the candle again and the end flares brighter for just a second before it goes black. I look up at the stars and go inside. We are ornaments.

The Guessing Pool for your birthday

Dawn: December 17, 3:00 a.m.

Tara: December 21, 5:00 p.m.

Grandpa Ron: December 17, ??

Grandma Joyce: December 17, ??

Aunt Davina: Too superstitious to guess

I spent the day getting ready for you. I am sitting between two opposites—feeling like I can't wait to see you, to hold you in my arms, and feeling that I have held you since I myself was born. I remember this feeling. It is all I ever wanted before I knew what it was. I celebrate by buying irises. They smell like my hopes for you in this life.

Shopping, going down the list today, I buy also the practical things that Tara and I were told we would need for delivering a baby at home: blankets, sheets, snacks and candles, heating pads and juice. I am always overwhelmed when I go to the store—the bright colors and endless choices make my vision tunnel and my mouth go dry. It has always been that way. Many times I go shopping very late at night so there are few people to add to the sensory chaos that is the modern grocery store. Even then it is difficult for me to navigate. If someone is in the aisle I need to shop in I go away until they leave. I almost never buy fish or pastries or deli food, since I would have to ask a worker for what I want and then I can't remember, being to overwhelmed by their direct gaze. If they are at all brusk it makes it even harder, as I feel under pressure to perform as a shopper . . .

But now I find myself standing in the store with the additional worry of you coming soon, making it worse because it is so important that I don't make any mistakes. I fade out of myself in the aisle with a hundred kind of drinks and think of water, simple.

I must have been standing there for a long time because a nice young woman who works at the store came to stand next to me. It takes me a moment to realize that she has spoken, that she is kind. She asks me if I need some help, and I don't know where to begin. I ask her which drink would look good to her if she was giving birth. She laughs. It is a pleasant and kind laugh, and I don't mind her standing next to me, even though I don't like people to stand next to me, especially strangers. My mind tells me that people are dangerous.

And they are. People fear each other. The flavor of distance seems to me to be how a community organizes itself. The codes of distance constitute the law—for the living and the dead. This is why people close the lid on the toilet when they sit down to talk to someone else in the bathroom, signaling that they don't intend to mark their territory in the midst of the other, and why men can't pick up and hold a crying child who is a stranger, why people smile and say hello more often when they are on a trail than when they are on a city street. They are always waiting for pardon to be what they are: strange and beautiful and terrible.

Our status is as enduring and fleeting as our dangerousness, and its truth rests on the final outcome of things, which we will never reach, and so we are suspended in our importance, drifting, with no law but the habits of nature. And I dream that ghosts are hospitable and welcome every living and dying thing and kiss all that is in between. We know where they are. We always know. We divine the future and the past; we shake and throw our own bones and read the signs.

Since ghosts can't hurt each other, I wonder if they divide their space and their labor like the organs of the body or the wheeling of the stars.

The store employee asks me again if I need help. I can't see her face because my vision is a tunnel. I sit in a cave, lost in the ice age when I'm like this. I close my eyes and imagine walking through this tunnel and out, as if it wasn't there, or climbing over it, perhaps digging under it. "Maybe," I think, my eyes pushed together tight, as if trying to dispel some bad dream, "I could just kick through it, kick and kick until the void without numbers gave up rebuilding itself and gave me my path back." My face relaxes as I open my eyes. I am determined to be . . . here . . . now.

The young woman puts her hand on my shoulder and leaves it there. I like this and that surprises me. She gives my shoulder a small squeeze and tells me she would like Gatorade. She puts one in my basket and I get five more.

When I come home I scrub the house and make the bed with clean sheets. I check to be sure I have the midwife's number by the phone. I rub Tara's shoulders and tell her she is beautiful. I ask her if there is anything I can do for her. She tells me, "Just be near." As usual, I take her too literally and walk behind her as she moves from room to room. She laughs. She squeezes my shoulder.

Expecting Teryk

A Near-Solstice Dream

It is the dark time just before dawn. High in the trees of a tiny copse surrounded by the tall blowing grass, the family begins to open their dark brown eyes to the soft call of the birds around them. From the holding comfort of their woven nests, the people stir, one by one. Reluctant to move, the people stretch and look toward the pale streaks of orange just cresting the distant mountains. The first rays of the sun glow on the hair that grows richly over their bodies and glints on their large teeth as they yawn and call to one another in the light.

The men of the group stretch simultaneously and step each from his nest. In their hands they already carry sturdy weapons of club and stone; favorites against a frightening, unpredictable world. Their one collective thought is to protect their families. They are fathers, grandfathers, great-grandfathers.

A strong older man, the leader of the leaders, unconsciously strokes the knotty club that he carries. It is polished from years of use, here and there pitted or scraped, the surviving stains of the blood of hunted or hunting animals still tracing victory and defeat.

The rousing women, tired mothers, grandmothers, great-grandmothers, in no hurry to race to meet the long day, ignore the men and contentedly play with the newly woken youngsters, tickling and dangling them in the air to evoke their soft pants of laughter. Siblings provoke each other into wrestling games that proceed down the trees and into the field.

The leaders survey the land and sniff at the air. The rest of the large family stops and imitates their motions, a chorus of wide noses on wide faces turned first this direction, then that, their curious eyes scanning right and left under shading brow ridges. Finally the older men start for the river in the center of their valley, followed closely by younger men. The mothers, the grandmothers, the great-grandmothers, and the children follow cautiously behind. Several young men circle around to follow the women and watch for danger from behind. The leader counts. Five grown men. Four mothers with ten children. Three young men. Men and women bound to other in love, men who have never bonded to women—the children's favorite uncles—and women who have bonded together, raising each other's children. $5 + 4 + 10 + 3 = 22$. Twenty-two people. It is a number the leader feels. It is more than a sum. It is a living memory of actions and emotions, because no one is one alone.

The rain has made the prairie muddy in spots, and the family stoops occasionally to pick up the insects that have crawled to the surface of the mud. A young mother responds to the begging hand of the tiny child on her back and gives him the small worm she had just pulled from the fast-drying ooze. As her son eats, the strengthening sun falls on his small shoulders.

The light pink skin under the sparse hair of his body is in contrast to the brown skin and dark hair of his mother. Most of the people look like his mother, but some are darker, some lighter. Many of the older people have silver hair, and the very oldest have white patches and places on their bodies where there is no hair at all. The boy's grandmother is one of the latter, and she walks near her granddaughter and her offspring, sometimes reaching toward her grandson to clean him, caress him, kiss him. Her wrin-

Expecting Teryk

kled face creases in joy as she grasps his hand. She always has a smile for him, for life, and the people love her.

As the people reach the edge of the river, some stop to drink from it, compressing their long, muscular lips to suck up the cool water. They raise their heads from time to time, alert to danger. After some time they settle into the ritual of slaking their deep thirst, listening to comforting sounds of the grassland around them.

The people's collective complacence is broken by an explosive roar as an animal breaks through the grass at the edge of the river trail. Children run to their mothers, who sweep them into the sea of tall grass close at hand, hiding. The men begin jumping, swinging their clubs and throwing river stones in a fury of rippling muscles, screams, and the odor of fear until the deadly presence retreats, turning to snarl and punctuate its reluctance to leave without carrying someone away.

After staying absolutely still to make certain that the threat has passed, the men shout for the people to congregate on the riverbank once again. With trepidation, mothers stand up to look over the tall grass and survey the area for themselves. Each family makes its way back to the river.

The traveling formation falls in together and starts out once again. As the afternoon grows hotter, the men lead the people to the shade of a copse of trees much like the one they had made their nests in the night before. Relieved from the heat and fear of the oppressive day, men and women relax in the shade while their children—whose memories of danger are short—play and explore expectantly, their hearts full of magic.

The little boy, under the watchful eye of his grandmother, has discovered that the rotten log he turned over in his play is full of larvae, and his grandmother and mother gather around it, biting off the ends of small twigs to dig out the fat, squirming grubs. With a gnarled, scaly hand, the pot-bellied grandmother expertly digs out a handful of grubs and puts them on a large leaf. She moves into better shade and chews the grubs, one at a time, with the worn stumps of her teeth as she watches her family from a distance.

The leader dozes peacefully in a soft circle of grass dappled with sunlight. Now and then he opens his eyes sleepily to benignly regard one of the several females and babies clustered around, making soft sounds of contentment. The people enjoy the heat of the passing afternoon, sleeping where they lie.

A cry . . . the leader opens his eyes. In one movement, the waking group turns toward the sound of crying. Grandmother's daughter had cried out and now covers her face with her hands. Grandmother is dead. Her grandson pulls at grandmother's lifeless arm, keening whimpers of distress at her still form. The leader comes close and sniffs at grandmother's mouth. He stares. The leaf with grubs on it lies by her side, two of the naked, defenseless forms still wiggling uselessly.

His face is still and sad. He knows grandmother will not walk with them anymore. In frustration he reaches up and breaks a branch from the tree overhead, waving it over the dead body. Joining him in his show of grief, grandmother's daughter rips handfuls of grass from the ground and throws them into the air with every muffled cry. The people around them shake off their stillness one by one and pull at the grass also, letting it fly. The grass gently falls, like rain, like tears, until much of grandmother's body disappears. The leader, his chest heaving and his living heart beating hard, lets the broken branch come to rest over what remains.

The sun is sinking low and looks flat across the field at the small band of people. Night is coming for everyone. Swimming through his numbness,

Expecting Teryk

the leader motions for the people to make ready for the darkness. People begin to climb the trees and weave the branches as they always do, making places to hide, places to keep them away from the cold ground, places to wait for the dawn of another wakened day. It is quiet.

The leader climbs into the branches closest to the earth and sits without preparing a place of safety. One of his children climbs into his lap. He encircles her with his arms and thinks about his past—being held—and about her future—holding another small child in her own arms. The grassland is completely still. The leader feels the wind blow against his face and in the last light he turns his gaze to the forest floor, where grandmother lies. He has known her his whole life, and now he will see her, hear her, feel her only in his mind. He will remember her. He will remember her because he is a man, because he is an animal, he is the earth and wind and water. He wonders whether the child in his arms will remember him. In a faint thought hard for him to hold, he wonders whether he, whether all the people who have died—the mothers, the fathers, the grandmothers, the grandfathers, the great-grandmothers and great-grandfathers—will be remembered by someone in this way. He thinks of his children and the children of the children of his great-grandchildren, a long line into a future he can't see.

He gives a last long call into the night.

PART 0

Being Born

December 18, 1998

I feel the world in every breath,
I live its life and die its death,
Its crying width and laughing breadth,
As above, below.

I struggle in its timeless grasp
And hear its ticking seconds rasp
Myself to flesh as Eve to asp,
My spirit wants to know.

I feel as baby and as stone
One half flower, one half bone,
The gem has hardened and has shown
The fossil mine to show.

My sister flew in yesterday and we picked her up outside Seattle to bring her to our home in Tacoma. I felt so relieved to have her here. Tara and Davina and I are so anxious to see you that we started talking about ways to induce labor, and I eventually made Tara an omelet with castor oil in it. We were all joking about it and being quite skeptical that anything would happen; additionally, it was the most disgusting thing we had ever seen, and we all grimaced as Tara ate every bite.

We were watching television several hours later when Tara winced. I saw it out of the corner of my eye.

195

"I think something is happening," she said as she leaned over painfully with her hand on her huge stomach. What happened was that she threw up over and over while having diarrhea at the same time. I held the bathroom garbage pail for her as she sat on the toilet, wishing she were anywhere else but where she was. She started having regular contractions. I picked up the phone with my hand shaking, unable to swallow. When the midwife picked up the phone, I told her that it was time. You were coming.

I put bottles of water into the refrigerator and neatly placed all of the things we would need around the room: towels, sheets, blankets, bowls, some small snacks. I lit a fire in the fireplace and sat back, crouching, watching. The wildman is coming.

The red warmth of the fire played a shadow theater across my mind as the crystal cold settled on the night outside. I remembered a story I had read, years ago, about the Yeti in the high Himalayan snows, the Tibetan "Yeh-Teh," derived from "Meh-Teh Kang-Mi," or, "the Powerful Man of the Snows." He is said in legends to have backward pointing feet, and perhaps, I think, it is because he is always going back where he came from.

In the story I thought of, several men were on a hunting trip when they discovered a cave; there they decided to pass the night. Eventually, all but one man had fallen asleep; and that man felt it would be safer to fall asleep outside, so he found a large tree to sleep beneath. Before long, the man saw a Yeti approach the cave. When the wildman of the Himalayas saw the men, the Yeti paused, then tore a small tree from its roots, trying to frighten the men away. Eventually he left when the fire was stirred. In another story a group of village women were alone during the absence of the hunting village men. The women heard strange noises throughout the night and awoke to find that the Yetis had placed huge boulders against the doors of their houses and they could not get out.

Expecting Teryk

I stirred the fire, I checked the doors, but my fear remained. I was scared of the enormity of you, approaching the cave, coming to me in the night, coming to stay, but there was nowhere to run but to you with open arms.

Soon Tara was having strong contractions and was in a lot of pain. She had lain in the bathtub for awhile because it made her feel better, but before long she was in too much pain to stay in and made her way, naked as the day she was born, to our bed and lay there. She was crying and moaning and asking for me to please help her. There was nothing I could do.

I didn't want to leave her, but I asked Davina to hold her for just a minute while I ran outside. As soon as I was outside, I threw up under the cold stars, suddenly aware of my smallness in the world and feeling my own acceleration through space. I threw up in our flowerbed near the back door. I hurried back in to find Davina sitting with her back against the wall and Tara leaning back on her in turn. As Davina turned her face to me I saw that she was pale and her eyes were wide. I had never seen her scared before. Tara was still asking for us to please help her.

I thought about a story I had heard once, a story about the first marathoner. An Athenian whose army won a battle in that city, he carried news of the victory, running twenty-six miles to Athens to announce the triumph they shared. When he arrived in Athens and was surrounded by the waiting, anxious people, he managed to say only one word—*victory*—and then fell dead. Watching Tara I suddenly knew that it was not of the victory of Athens that he spoke; it was, by that time, his own that he declared. He had made it.

Your mother ran her race. She ran it for ten hours, over twenty-six miles of her trust in her own body, in her love for me, and in her love for you. It was a trust and a run that put her panting over lost fields, crying in lost ancestral caves, in the middle of a darkness I will never know in this life, in the darknesses of mothers, in the darknesses of the end, in the darknesses of the beginning.

At 4:11 a.m. she screamed and gave one mighty push. Because the sea that surrounded you as you grew surrounded you still, you burst into the world on a tidal wave of salt and tears, tears of happiness and the forgetfulness of pain. Tara forgot her pain, Davina forgot her pain, and I also; the pain of a lifetime, the pain of a deathtime, the pain of not feeling pain until it is late and the hour of a new start reminded me only that I had had a life before, but that it was now gone.

Dimly, I heard a voice tell me silently that I would not be alone anymore, that I had people, that I had you, here and now, that I had evolved backwards, that I had a culture to dig up where it rested in the light and a family that I had always belonged to—it is written in me.

I opened my eyes to see you carefully lifted, an unusual artifact from the ground that had cradled it, and placed on Tara's chest. You opened your eyes and found us. We found you. You seemed the kind of precious thing that anthropologists look for all their short lives—something significant and millions of years old. A long, brown, skinless key to our ancestry, a spliced film inside out, a memory bone.

I have been digging you up since I was born. You are my soul.

You took several small and quiet breaths. Everyone cried small and quiet tears. We all knew, though no one said, that we had brought you into the world and that you would, many years from now, hold the hands in the room, each in turn, and show us how to go back from where you had come.

On this day, December 18, in 1859, an English writer, Francis Thompson, was born. He wrote:

> *All things by immortal power,*
> *Near and Far*
> *Hiddenly*
> *To each other linked are,*
> *That thou canst not stir a flower*
> *Without troubling a star.*

You are here. You are here.

Epilogue

I sit beneath the frozen sky
And lift my face
For one long cry,

My voice to mountains lends its song
The song is old
The singer young,

Its words are written on a stone
Beyond the snow
Within the bone,

I learned it at the edge of night,
I found its notes
With second sight,

It has no name that mortals know,
It is not sung
Where mortals go.

Anthropologist Marjorie Halpin tells us that according to Gitksa Indian tradition, only a person without fault could see the Wild One. And when it calls, a person is obligated to follow as the sun goes around four times, whereupon he or she will come to pi'kis—the wildwoman. The person must then take her child, who will then magically appear to be human. I heard the call when my Teryk was born.

After Teryk was born, the midwife told us that his cord had never finished growing properly, that at one end—the end closest to his body and farthest from Tara's—it had no protection at all. She told us that he could easily have died; her words remind me still that my son belongs not to me but to a million chances, to a hidden history and happy endings, perhaps; he belongs to himself. The fact that he is here helps me melt into the world, into my own fate, like a slowly dissolving communion, its redemption now on my tongue, written in life's wine. His coming, his life, was and is my atonement, my at-one-ment, something I will lose and never lose.

I will never have amnesty from my love for him.

I expected to have to say these things and say them this eloquently when I adopted my son so that I would never have to know the pain of the world not seeing him as mine. I worried that the judge would think me unfit. I had heard that many judges wouldn't let gay people adopt children, even if they were there from their beginnings, bringing them into the world. The arguments are religious, or social—I'm not sure what the real reason is. We were told that we needed to travel to King County, the county neighboring us to the north, in order to maximize our chances of getting a sympathetic judge. It was by no means certain even then that I would have no trouble.

Expecting Teryk

I could be considered unfit because I was odd, neurologically different. I was aware that many people in the world don't think that disabled people should have kids. I still hear the words of people raised by autistics, saying that their parents were selfish, that they hurt them, yelled at them just for being children, that they had been viewed as malfunctioning machines instead of small ones in need of love and tenderness. I remembered the words saying that their autistic parents had never let them stretch, that they had been contained, embarrassed in public when their parents acted strangely.

I also remembered the words of the children who had found their autistic parents honest to a fault, steady and predictable, creative and imaginative . . . and loving. That was the parent I would be.

I rehearsed a thousand times in my mind the way I would not waver when I looked into the judge's eyes, a feat so hard for me, and a thousand times I rehearsed what I would say about my love for him; how I would pick him up when he fell, how I would tell him I had few answers, how I would tell him my dreams, how to save him I would fly into the sun, his face my last thought.

When the time came, though, the judge asked us all into the courtroom without preamble. My mother and sister sat in the front row, and Tara and I, Teryk in our arms, approached the bench. The judge looked at the paperwork briefly and then at Tara and me. She had to ask which one of us was adopting him because he looks more like me than anyone else in the world.

When I had told her that it was me, she cleared her throat and asked, "Do you understand that you will be this child's parent from this day on?"

"Yes." I said it quietly.

"Do you understand that you will be financially responsible for this child?"

"Yes."

"Are you prepared to offer this child religious education?"

"Yes." Where was my heart? My words? I forced myself to look at her and hoped she would see all of it within me. I was starting to cry.

"By the authority vested in me I hereby grant the petition for adoption." She banged her gavel. It was all over in less than five minutes. I turned to smile at my mom and my sister, at Tara. They were all crying, too. Overcome, we all turned to leave the courtroom. I heard the voice of the judge behind me.

"Aren't you going to take my picture with him?" She was smiling and warm now. Tara and I hurried up and put Teryk in her arms. We stood beside her. My mom, with shaking hands, took a photograph. The judge smiled at me. "I remember what it's like," she said.

The first time Teryk ever smiled, he was in the back seat of the car. I was getting ready to put him in his car seat, and he peeped over the edge of the seat to see our two dogs in the back, behind him. They were looking at him through the safety grille and smiling, and he smiled back. I never really had to teach him to be kind like that, to see the beauty and importance of the living things around him. When he was first walking, he would come near to an animal—one he knew, or one that was new to him—and he would squat down and wait for it to come to him. He would pat it softly. I have a memory of him doing this, surrounded by bright sunshine, looking back at me as if to say, "Isn't it good to be alive?" This memory and sunshine are the same to me, and the way my memory works is a blessing when the sun is out and I can see his smiling face, his tiny, patting hand on the cat's head, just like it was the day I was standing there, with him tiny and full of wonder.

Life is a thing he loves. This is as terrible a thing as it is wondrous. When he was trying to save a spider at the library when he was three, urging it to climb onto Tara's hand to put it outside, some teenage boys came over and killed it, stepped on it right in front of him, telling him they had just saved his life—they were certain that the wolf spider was a brown recluse. He cried for days about the death of the spider and his helplessness to save it. The memory still bothers him. A year later I looked out through the window of the back door to see him staring intently at the lid of our hot tub. He began to carefully touch his fingers to the place where he stared, cup them, and walk slowly over to the bush near the deck. Over and over he did this. When I came out to see what he was doing, he proudly showed me that he was escorting baby spiders, the size of pinpoints, over to the bush one by one so that they could find a better place to live.

He has come home from school crying because he is different. Through his tears he tells me that he cares about things the other kids don't care about. When I ask him to tell me more, he says simply, "I am responsible." He doesn't want to say any more. I hug him and tell him I understand.

I think of so many stories that have this ending. He took me by the hand and led me to the yard one day to show me his roly-poly farm. He had filled his yellow bucket with leaves and dirt, food from the compost bin, a little lid with water, and some bark for the little gray bugs to hide under.

"What's that?" I asked, kneeling and pointing to a broad stick leaning against the side of the bucket. It was a ladder so that the roly-polies could leave when they got tired of being there.

When he was four he asked me where suffering comes from. I told him that there were many ideas about that, but that most people believed that suffering came from having a brain that was capable of processing feelings of pain and discomfort. He thought about that and then said, "So we shouldn't eat things with brains then, should we?" I told him that some very fine people had come to this conclusion and that some very fine people decided that it was ok to eat animals, too. I told him to decide for himself. He did.

There is joy in his way of looking at things. My son has told me, as he has looked out on a winter world, that there are three laughters. Bunnies, he says, are the laughter of God. Plants, he says, are the laughter of Mother Nature. The mountain's laughter is snow. He believes that because whales are several times greater than us in size, their thoughts are several times greater as well. He thinks that imaginary friends are just people that other people forgot to play with.

My son, now six years old, asks me the larger questions: When will I die? When will you die? What is life? What is death? He asks the questions that each of us will ask for the rest of our lives and perhaps beyond: What is God? How do you live a good life? What is beauty? He asks with an intensity that anticipates his own growing, his own possible fatherhood, his eventual passing, his afterlife as an ancestor.

I like to believe that he gets all these things from me. Perhaps he absorbed them through his unfinished cord, the invisible part that was tied to me. Perhaps he got them from all the wild things that went before. I fear and smile to know what his life will be like because of them. I know it will be a good life, a deep life. He will feel.

Expecting Teryk

The other day my son and I were waking up in the same bed, listening to classical music on the radio. The third movement of Edgar Bainton's *A Kentish Suite* was playing, slow and bittersweet, like this season, like this life. My son rolled over to me, opening his sleepy eyes and looking deep into mine for a long time. Still listening to the music he said, "This sounds like forever."

His finished book is on the shelf.